# YOUR AFTERNOON MENTOR

# YOUR AFTERNOON MENTOR

Real World, Real Clear Advice on Landing
and Leading a Life in Senior Leadership

———————————

# KEVIN SALCIDO

**HOUNDSTOOTH**
PRESS

Paperback ISBN: 978-1-5445-2863-2
eBook ISBN: 978-1-5445-2864-9

# CONTENTS

# INTRODUCTION

———————————

Have you ever met a self-assured person in your organization who appeared destined for a role in senior leadership?

Spend some time with me, and I'll tell you about people like Aaron.

I met him at a consumer products company. A few years older than me, he already managed a significant region of the country, and he looked the part. His clothes of exceptional quality fit his athletic frame and always appeared neatly pressed. His haircut said "Marines meet Hollywood"—a brush job conveying both authority and accessibility. I can't say if he amounted to a great leader because I did not work for him, but I found him quite charismatic. I can't say whether he was unusually smart—he used a lot of trendy B-school management speak—but he sure could hold an audience. I did know, in our company's up-or-out culture, he was rising quickly. I saw his name recently in a *Forbes* article listing the CEOs of the largest companies in America. He made it.

Have you worked with a person who served as a good lieutenant but could not break through to becoming a general? Could this person be you?

Give me a moment, and I'll tell you about Lewis, my former colleague.

We worked together at a different company during a time when I led a difficult search for a VP of production. Lewis had been doing a great job in an interim role. With us for years, he knew our equipment and processes cold. Though he always appeared simply unpolished in style and dress, his people loved him. We all did. He was great company, though not at all at ease speaking in front of groups. Aware of himself as the strongest internal candidate, he didn't come forward to us to press his case. I suggested removing the interim tag as the search dragged, but my boss thought we could not put him in front of our board. We finally found someone, and Lewis quietly moved on to another company a few months later.

Buy me lunch, and I'll explain the importance of networking and actively managing your career.

Regina thoroughly impressed me when I met her. She told me it had been her goal for a number of years to work for us. She read about our mission and our rising profile, thought about her current status—comfortable but stagnant—and decided to actively market herself to us. She lit up her network in our industry until our hiring unit often recognized her name. She made a point to focus on developing relationships after she joined us. Right away, management saw her as a person who could move things. She exuded potential.

When we next meet, remind me to tell you about the time I saw a vice president pull the pin on a career grenade and catch the blast in his face.

Gregory ran a major and profitable division of a retail company. Creative and innovative, he responded well to financial incentives, so we usually paid him a maximum bonus. He lived large, bought the latest toys, and loved to gamble. One day, he was swept up in an online prostitution sting reported in the press. Say goodbye to Gregory.

I gathered dozens of these anecdotes during my more than thirty years in human resources management, working near the top of major organizations. I've observed how some people make it to senior levels, while others—of equal talent, effort, and devotion to their work—languish. I've seen how understanding the nature of the senior leadership role expands and extends careers. Sadly, I've also watched good people self-destruct because they could not manage their emotions or appetites.

On a more positive note, I also learned how cultivating five attitudes will result in sustained career success in the executive suite.

You may be at the start of your working life. You have your education and formal training, and you're brimming with optimism and drive. Yet it's unlikely anyone ever sat you down to explain the basics of navigating the journey and maximizing your professional potential. It's unlikely you've ever asked. I completed my career trek and learned success at the senior level is not as mystical or elusive as it appears from where you sit today. I want to share these lessons with you.

This is why I wrote *Your Afternoon Mentor*.

I targeted this book to those in early- to midcareer roles looking to break through to senior management. Its purpose? To take some of the serendipity out of your career arc and give you insights into how to earn notice for a larger role, grow into an executive position, and keep your career on a solid footing until you, and only you, decide to leave it.

Though not a traditional book about executive presence, I will talk about how to project confidence and competence to others.

Leadership is not the focus of this book. You already own several dozen of those books and probably did not read past the third chapter in any one of them. I will, however, spend time on the basics of effectively managing people and organizations because that's what the role demands.

Some books go deep into seeking happiness and fulfillment at work. That's not my area of interest or expertise; plus, I think they call it "work" for a reason. I will definitely tell you what workplace, and private, behaviors to avoid and embrace. The discussion will include what to expect during the course of your senior leadership career and how you should respond. You'll receive a taste of how rewarding an executive life can be.

Though I spent the happiest and most productive years of my career at a great university stuffed full with wonderful scholars, I did not create an academic journal here. I have conducted no experiments on live subjects, reviewed no large data sets, nor subjected my suggestions to peer review. I offer you no new methods or models.

Think of *Your Afternoon Mentor* as a more-experienced and wiser person with whom you have a casual but meaningful mentoring relationship—someone you hope will share advice as you explore taking on higher-visibility jobs.

You don't want to hear buzzwords, soaring rhetoric, or pithy platitudes. You want clear advice in clear language about how they did it, how they lasted, and what they experienced along the way—with maybe a few stories thrown in to keep things interesting.

I intend to give you such counsel.

I will move along at a good pace. Though you've heard almost everything I am going to tell you before, I gather it for you in one place and in order.

As I visit concepts such as presence, communication skills, emotional intelligence, or creating a strategic vision, know I am hitting highlights and giving you an illustration of why these things are so important. You can find an abundance of information on these topics everywhere. I hope what you see here provokes you to explore more.

I also suggest a few exercises to help bring these points to life. I encourage you to try them with me because they can help crystalize how you look at things, how you look at yourself, and how you identify opportunities for improvement.

You may notice I use the terms "executive leadership" and "senior leadership" interchangeably. This is because the lexicon may differ by industry.

You already observed that I like stories, and you will hear many more. My attorneys want you to know every tale is true, though I changed names, titles, organizations, and time lines to avoid embarrassing anyone I encountered in my career.

Are you ready to learn about landing and leading a life in senior leadership?

Are you ready to spend an afternoon with me?

# PART I

# BE NOTICED AS SOMEONE WITH POTENTIAL

---

t is not as difficult as you imagine to gain attention as someone with upward potential in an organization.

Think of a person in a leadership role you always admired and would like to emulate. This person can be somebody you worked with, somebody from your various social circles, or even a national political or media figure.

What appealing physical traits does this person display?

What do you find so memorable about the way they communicate and engage with others?

How does this person carry themselves? What tangible or intangible qualities project confidence, competence, and even power?

I know your thoughts because they are pretty common. You recalled somebody who always looks professional, healthy, and emotionally and physically fit. This sets them apart. Someone engaged, in the moment, and energetic. You remembered an approachable person. Something about this person exudes trustworthiness and makes you believe they care about you. They exemplify confidence but without a cocky air. They understand and shape their environment. This person knows the answers or, at least, grasps the right questions.

These characteristics are commonly referred to as "executive presence."

The good news: every one of these attributes or behaviors can be learned. The person you thought of came out of the womb as naked and inexperienced as you did. They were not born with any natural advantages over you. They took what the universe gave them, invested in themselves, learned through trial and error what worked for them, and never stopped striving to improve.

I break the concept of executive presence into five broad areas:

- Appearance

- Communication style

- Swagger

- Authenticity

- The ability to connect and leverage relationships

Before digging deeper into these dimensions of executive presence, let's look at our natural thought patterns and how they impact conclusions we draw about people we meet in daily life.

# CHAPTER 1

# IMPORTANCE OF PERCEPTIONS

---

Any discussion of how others perceive you has to begin with how you perceive others.

Psychologists tell us our brains are a messy gumbo of biases that inform almost everything we do and every decision we make. The following four are the most pertinent to our discussion of executive presence.

**Confirmation Bias.** A critical bias to be aware of in others and to overcome in yourself. Confirmation bias is our tendency to select information in our environment, or from other people, that supports a belief we have and to ignore evidence refuting the belief.

If I believe I like you and you are good person, I will continue to select signals from you validating my affection for you. I'm also likely to ignore any evidence that I decided you are a good person prematurely.

Alternatively, I may draw a conclusion you are a threat or an incompetent person, and I will ignore evidence signaling maybe you are all right after all. Any innocuous thing you do will only reinforce my negative perception.

Understanding confirmation bias is so important because if you get off on the right foot with someone and they decide to like and trust you, you will have them on your side for a long time—unless you truly mess up. If you experience a poor start with someone, you are challenged to overcome their first impression.

**Similarity Bias.** This bias shows up in a different way. We are predisposed to surround ourselves with, and develop an affinity for, those most like us. This comes into play when we encounter people of similar race, age, or gender. It may also trigger when we share a common nonphysical trait, like having a degree from the same school, hailing from the same region of the country, or sharing a hobby or interest.

I remember as a younger manager drawing conclusions about older people in the workplace, thinking maybe they were a little out of touch or hanging around past their prime. As I am now more senior, I have to fight the tendency to see some, but not all, younger people as quaintly inexperienced and vaguely naïve. Both perceptions are terribly inaccurate.

This is similarity bias in full bloom.

It matters because if you are the most dissimilar person in a room or organization, you will need to work harder to earn acceptance.

**Self-Regard Bias.** Related to the above, we all give ourselves too much credit in certain aspects of our lives. We think ourselves better looking than we actually are. Of course, we've been gifted with a larger brain than most. Our opinions are, naturally, the right opinions. Our innate expertise at work, or at picking the dinner wine for the table, is unassailable. Everything we accomplished was through the dint of our own hard work, while others relied on luck for their success.

There is nothing wrong with a sturdy ego because it's the foundation for confidence, which we've already learned is a critical element of executive presence. You will not likely be successful without a healthy serving of it.

Yet we often let this sense of superiority obscure how we see others we encounter. The brain whirs into action and assesses whether they meet our standards. Not because they are tall or short, Black or white, old or young, Ivy League or state-school educated. No, we make this evaluation for no other reason than they are not us, and we are pretty special.

While you are mentally sniffing at these people from your high perch, what do you think they're doing to you?

**Unconscious or Implicit Bias.** This bias is a bit more controversial. This refers to our tendency to attribute positive or negative characteristics to different racial, ethnic, gender, age, or other demographic groups. We make these associations because of things we heard about various groups growing up at home, messages from the media—pay attention to how minorities are portrayed in old movies and TV shows—or other life experiences.

Early in my career, I dealt with a disciplinary issue involving a recent immigrant from the then-crumbling, communist Eastern Europe. This older person worked in a menial role, which signaled something negative to me. I also assumed a lower level of intelligence because of his thick accent, an ignorant but common reaction. When he told me he held a master's degree in electrical engineering from a top university in Poland, I learned a lesson about implicit bias—about making assumptions about people.

Even as an individual in a so-called majority group—like a white male, for example—people make assumptions about you for no other reason than your membership in the group.

Remember, people always watch you, like you watch them, and they come to lightning-quick conclusions.

Being familiar with these biases helps you overcome them when you encounter them—and you will always encounter them.

Let's dig into the elements of executive presence.

# CHAPTER 2

# YOUR APPEARANCE

---

While I was still fairly new in HR and with my employer for less than a year, the vice president of my department—a great guy who still serves as a mentor—took a liking to me and gave me a slight pay bump. Not really a promotion, just something to recognize me. After I thanked him for the unexpected increase, he told me, "Maybe now you can afford to buy pants with a crease."

Ouch. Point taken. Crank up your dress game, Kevin.

People always watch you.

It cannot be overstated the message dress sends to you and others. You must understand this if you want others to notice you.

When you dress well, you feel better. You feel more confident and in control. Studies show you are more productive and vigorous. Dressing well kicks off a virtuous cycle as you begin to look into other avenues for self-improvement. All things being equal, the best-dressed person in the room usually receives the most respect and deference. You'll never have to worry about feeling out of place in any setting.

With all these many benefits, why don't people dress better? I'm looking at you, men.

Dressing, like eating and breathing, is something we do every day of our lives. After a certain point, it becomes rote, like taking the same streets to work every morning. We give little conscious thought to what we wear. Time moves, the calendar clicks, and the wardrobe ages and goes out of style. Where did the crease go?

The answer here: be more mindful about this important aspect of your professional persona.

Try this exercise.

Sometime in the next week, and every year on your birthday, go through your closet with a critical eye, and cull anything you wear to work that looks aged, worn, discolored, or stained; does not fit well; or simply fell out of style. Put those clothes in a bag—double bag cargo or denim shorts—and drop them off at a donation station. This alone brings the routine act of dressing back into your consciousness.

## THE WELL-DRESSED MAN

I will not lay out a dress code because standards differ by industry and company. Instead, consider these few general nuggets of advice.

**Shoes.** Keep them newer and shined. Men generally don't need to own multiple pairs, like women do, so spend more money on quality. It shows. Plus, you receive a return on investment because you can recondition or resole them many times during their life cycle.

**Buy well-fitting clothes.** Your body changes, so the thirty-inch waistline and fifteen-and-a-half-inch neckline may be things of the past. More optimistically, maybe you lost weight and should show some physique. Resize whenever you repurchase.

**Change up your source of clothing.** Likely, you've shopped for work clothes at the same stores for years, so try a new place when you refresh. Expect a pleasant surprise from items you never knew existed.

**Keep your work-wardrobe colors neutral.** Neutral clothes are easier to mix and match and less likely to go out of style than patterns or prints. You can afford to spend more on quality since you need to buy less.

**You're better off with one good suit than two cheap ones.** A poor-quality suit can boomerang on you. Instead of finding people impressed with your style, you'll notice them wincing at your lame suit. Men don't wear suits often in most industries. So spend more than you want to on one or two great suits built to last, or that can be altered over time.

**Accessories.** Not only for women. Invest in a nice belt, and keep it looking new. Buy and wear a nice watch. No need to go crazy. Plenty of nice options cost around $300. An understated bracelet or necklace adds some style.

## THE WELL-DRESSED WOMAN

Having never dressed as a professional female, I did the next best thing: scoured the internet for tips. It provided a consensus for women's attire to set yourself apart.

**Shoes.** Good-quality, leather-looking pumps with heels no higher than three inches. Stick to basic colors like black, brown, and navy blue. Avoid open-toed or sling-back styles. As with men, invest in better quality, and keep them in good shape.

**Blouses and tops.** Neutral colors or soft prints work best in cotton, silk, and other natural fabrics. Avoid anything sheer or low-cut. Don't forget to resize when you reload this part of your wardrobe, and only show as much of your form as you are comfortable with.

**Skirts.** Wear them knee-length or at least long enough to cover your thighs when seated.

**Suits or pantsuits.** Again, it is best to invest in fewer but better suits because you won't wear them every day, and you will stand out when you do. Most experts recommend wool or quality wool blends on the darker end of the color palette, with classic styles preferred to overly trendy.

**Hair and makeup.** Not going near this other than to suggest you do whatever maximizes your confidence level.

**Jewelry and accessories.** Most advice here says to stay muted, and keep rings to engagement or wedding bands. Keep earrings smaller and fairly inconspicuous. Good-quality belts should match shoes. Stylish leather portfolios or datebooks can also make a good impression.

These general guidelines have not varied much through cyclical changes in tastes and trends. Stay within them, and create a professional look of your own. Know you send a signal through dress. You want the message to be positive and powerful.

Revisit the person you thought of at the beginning of this section. Something about their dress probably stuck with you. The best advice is to imitate those who impress you.

## PROJECT HEALTH AND WELLNESS

Have you ever watched a senior military officer interviewed on a news show? To me, these incredibly accomplished people exude health and wellness. Though older and deeper in their careers, I never saw one who looked bedraggled or hungover, or one who coughed up a lung. They looked like they hit the gym at four thirty every morning.

What makes a healthy and fit person so appealing?

Again, this may go back to the way our brains are wired. Healthy-looking people project strength, energy, and confidence, which definitely catches the eye. Their clothes fit better. The bounce in their step is more apparent. They appear cooler and smarter.

The first thing you say to a person you've not seen in a while but who clearly has been working out is "You look great!"

Not "You look better than usual," but "You look great!"

Few of us are blessed with a tall, lean, and athletic build. Studies show these people tend to do better romantically and financially in life. No fair. Some of us grew up in this world… short. Others are big-boned and will never have a lithe body, no matter how hard they work out. Many people must manage chronic health conditions every day.

But everyone can improve on what nature gave them by exercising more, eating better, staying hydrated, and managing restorative sleep. These lifestyle choices have nothing to do with genetics or body type.

Whenever my physical activity drops, it shows up right away in my energy level. Same when I do not sleep well. You will survive being out of shape and groggy, but it makes it harder to thrive and be productive. The people who thrive and are productive earn notice, and others naturally gravitate to them.

> So why aren't you exercising more? No time? Look at the app on your phone telling you how much screen time you average per day. You have the time.

Expect to spend more time talking about physical and emotional wellness later "this afternoon." In the meantime, think critically and honestly about the ways your health, or lack thereof, is impacting how those around you perceive you. Decide on the changes you can make now to improve all areas of your health and wellness.

## YOUR HANDSHAKE

My friend had a direct connection to the Bill Clinton White House and introduced me to the then-president after a reelection campaign event in Phoenix. As he stepped forward to extend his hand, I was struck by his height, about six-foot-two, and his apparent eagerness to meet me—feigned, I'm sure. He looked me in the eye, extended a hand the size of a small catcher's mitt, repeated my name, gave my hand two firm pumps, and held the grip a half second longer than I expected.

A jolt of electricity went through my arm. Part was attributed to meeting the chief executive, but part was his ability to convey a sincere interest in the moment. Regardless of what you think of Clinton's politics or personal life, no one doubts his legendary charisma. I experienced it that day.

A handshake is not technically part of your appearance, but it does play a key role in establishing how people react to you.

Let's do an exercise.

Take a moment, and find a friend or significant other to help out here. Act like you are introducing yourself to this person for the first time. Make your grip noticeably weak and your shaking motion flaccid and unremarkable. Avoid eye contact as you mumble your name. Seriously, do this.

You will find the experience forgettable, if not downright embarrassing.

Follow the Clinton template, and introduce yourself again. This time,

- Stand and smile.

- Square off with the other person.

- As you do this, pull your shoulder blades together and slightly raise your chin.

- Extend your palm to theirs.

- Make a conscious effort to make your grip slightly firmer than the other person's.

- Look the person in the eye, and tell them your name, repeat their name, or both.

- Pump their hand two or three times while offering a sincere "Pleased to meet you."

- Hold the grip a half second longer, all while maintaining eye contact.

Ask your partner if they experienced a difference. Ask yourself if you felt more powerful.

Shaking hands is a routine social nicety. Break the routine. Stand out. Especially when meeting somebody for the first time.

# CHAPTER 3

# YOUR COMMUNICATION STYLE

---

Let's move on the second key element of executive presence: how you communicate with others.

People assess your intelligence and competence, your status, your commitment to the moment, and your mood by how you communicate. We all have our own unique patterns that shape how those perceptions are formed. For example, you can control how you dress, project wellness, or shake someone's hand. You can modify these patterns to your advantage when cognizant of them.

## THE NONVERBAL

Think of how often you've entered an elevator and encountered somebody with their head tilted down, their shoulders hunched, and their nose buried in their phone. Think of how often you've walked into a meeting of participants slouched in their chairs, on their phones, and who didn't look up when you entered.

This happens at work daily.

You'll find nothing memorable or interesting about these people. They do not project any kind of power in these poses. They are disconnected from those around them. Nothing about them makes you want to follow them. They are wallpaper.

Don't be wallpaper.

Nonverbal communication is an interesting field. For our purpose, which is for you to earn notice, use body posture as the most-effective way to convey a forceful persona.

I have often heard communication experts say to "take up your space" when standing in a professional setting. This sounds like a fuzzy concept, so interpret it in your own way. I attempt to do this by:

- Keeping my shoulders back. I have a natural tendency to hunch, so I fight it simply by staying aware of it.

- Keeping my chin up off my chest and my eyes looking forward in a public setting.

- Slowly scanning the environment with my eyes so I don't look worried or fixated on something.

- Keeping an optimistic and eager expression.

- Putting some purpose in my stride.

- Staying off my phone.

Similarly, the way you present yourself sitting in a meeting conveys authority—or not.

- If sitting in an adjustable chair, discreetly lift it up an inch or so.

- Keep your feet flat on the floor.

- Do not collapse into your chair; you give your power away the moment you do this.

- Avoid crossing your arms or pushing your chair back from the table. These are unmistakable signs you don't care or, worse, you think you know it all.

- Make eye contact with those around you.

- Give a subtle greeting or nod to new attendees.

- Stay off your phone.

Go back to the person you thought of at the beginning of this section. This person does not slouch through life with their face three inches away from a phone screen.

Neither should you.

## SPEAKING SKILLS

*"Ask not what your country can do for you—ask what you can do for your country."*

*—President John F. Kennedy, January 1961*

Um, okay.

You have to continually improve your verbal skills if you want to advance your career. Your ability to express yourself becomes part of your identity quickly in an organization. As people assess your competence by how you dress and carry your physical self, they make the same calculation—probably more so—when words start tumbling out of your mouth.

They decide if you are smart, interesting, and deserving of their attention. It is no more complicated than this.

Confirmation bias.

A great way to earn notice in an organization is to actively seek opportunities to speak in front of groups. This is one of the best marketing tools available to you because it broadcasts your competence, and confidence, to a larger number of people. If you can pull it off with energy and enthusiasm, you will supercharge your advancement, especially if you have the right people in the audience.

A well-worn trope tells us people fear speaking in front of others only slightly less than they fear death. I don't know if it's true, but I do know it is an unnatural skill. Like every skill, speaking in front of a group is something to learn, refine, and perfect. You only have to devote the time and energy to it.

You can delve deep into this topic. You don't have to look far to find articles; online courses; webinars; or all-day, in-person public-speaking training programs. Toastmasters International still leads in the niche, so you can also check it out.

You know where the resources are, so let me offer some of my tips on speaking in professional settings or in front of groups:

- Many of our number labor under the fallacious misapprehension that utilizing polysyllabic words telegraphs that erudition and uncommon verbal acumen and agility are the ultimate indicators of superior cerebral capacity. Don't buy it. You will not pull this off. Always use the simplest terms possible when both speaking and writing. People will not think less of you.

- Avoid the tendency to rush when speaking in a small setting or in front of a group. I am not at all glib when speaking: words do not roll off my tongue, and I have a slight stutter. So I always make an effort to speak a half beat more slowly. Rushing also makes you appear unsure of yourself. It can lead you into a verbal blind alley where your audience focuses more on how you are going to rescue yourself than your presentation points.

- Along those lines, vary pacing. Learn how to use pauses for effect.

- Vary your pitch. Nobody likes a monotonous speaker. It makes you unapproachable.

- You probably, ya'know, have a verbal tic. It's, like, we all do. Ask a trusted colleague to identity it for you.

- Make it a point to speak more loudly than the person you follow on the program. This injects energy and puts people on notice you are a person who must be listened to.

- Drop your voice an octave when you want to emphasize a point. For some reason, it always brings credibility. This is not the same thing as saying you must have a masculine voice.

- I like to see people use hand gestures to make a point. I think it is effective.

Now, go to YouTube and search for "JFK ask not what your country can do for you…"

He did everything we discussed in thirty seconds. He kept his language simple, he paced himself, he paused, he used a varied but firm voice, and he made perfect hand gestures. This was a good line in his inauguration speech, but there were better ones. This quote lives in history because of how he delivered it.

Here are few more things I want you to know about speaking in a professional setting or in front of groups.

Never try to wing it. Ever. When asked to make a few comments at an event, or introduce a presentation, always jot down three to five items to mention—no more. Use an index card you can keep discreetly in the palm of your hand. This will have people thinking you are brilliant because you speak extemporaneously. The reality is you knew what you would say all along.

Don't believe the above is important? Think of the best man who made a fool of himself by making a toast at a wedding you attended because he came unprepared and rambled. You spent the rest of the night avoiding him at the bar because you were embarrassed for him. You talked about what an idiot he was on the way home. We all know him. Don't be him.

When asked to make a formal presentation, always show up early enough to explore the lay of the land. Familiarize yourself with the technology. Make sure your slides work. Make sure you know where the tripping hazards lie.

Don't speak from behind the podium. This is boring. You don't see any TED Talks delivered from behind a podium.

Keep things brief when you make public comments. It does not matter how proficient you are on a topic; you will lose your audience after eight to ten minutes. This is true even if you have a PowerPoint slide deck, which we all know should offer short bullet points. If you must go past ten minutes, look for ways to engage the audience, like asking for questions or doing a brief exercise.

Every time you speak in public, go back to the basics of dress, grooming, and posture. Chin up. Energy always.

Finally, and this is critical in verbal communication and public speaking, don't forget the biases discussed earlier. It is not fair, I did not cause it, and I sense it is changing, but women and minority group members must be extra proficient in this area to elicit the same level of credibility as a white man in the same position. They simply must.


## YOUR COMMUNICATION STYLE

I worked with a smart and successful CFO who could have served in the same role at a larger company or maybe even as CEO.

Interacting with others at the obligatory corporate or employee events was not his thing. This always mystified me because he was a delightful guy one-on-one. Yet he was frank about this. He did not like it.

I understand. Making small talk can be an annoyance when you're not in the mood, or if it does not come naturally to you. Not everyone can be an extrovert.

You limit yourself, however, if you can't engage sincerely with people of all walks of life at all levels of an organization.

You need to develop a public persona to earn notice as someone with growth potential. You can shape and polish it if you take a deliberate approach.

Be vibrant. I mentioned energy several times already, and you will hear it mentioned more. Strive to inject vibrancy into your interactions with people. You can do this in a variety of ways.

First, make it your goal to find common ground in personal interactions, especially if it is with someone you don't know well.

Look for points of connection. When you walk into someone's office, scan their desk for mementos. Scan their walls for pictures or awards. Displaying these items at work tells you they are proud of these aspects of their lives. They will want to talk about them.

Is there a model sailboat or airplane on their desk? Ask them if they sail or fly. Is there evidence of military service? Ask about it. Are they displaying a picture of the Colosseum? Ask if they liked Rome. The clues are always there if you look.

On a Monday or Tuesday, should you need to fill empty space in a conversation, ask the person what they did over the past weekend. On a Wednesday, ask them how their week is going so far. Thursday or Friday, ask them what plans are on deck for the coming weekend.

Notice you are not doing the heavy lifting in these conversations. You make the prompts and keep things moving. Remember, people like talking about themselves. We like attention, and we like the people who give it to us.

On the other side of the coin, be a good conversation partner.

Do this by staying in the moment and giving the person your full attention. Make eye contact, and don't scan the room for others to talk to while chatting with someone. People notice and can find it offensive.

Show a willingness to engage. If you close yourself off to people too quickly or abruptly, you will not gain a reputation as someone quiet, aloof, or mysterious. You will gain a reputation as someone that acts like a jerk.

People always watch you.

By contrast, don't dominate or show off. We are all certain of the rightness of our opinions and beliefs about the world, but this does not mean others are enamored with them, too. Make points, and move on. If somebody differs with you during the course of nonbusiness-related conversation, where not a lot is at stake, let them differ. It is their right.

Use brief stories and anecdotes. I am trying to work a story into every chapter of this book because it keeps things interesting and makes points more relatable.

Most stand-up comics spend a year or so developing a fifteen-minute set of material. You should also develop a repertoire of crisp, and proven, stories to deploy in different settings with select people.

Speaking of comedians, humor is one of the best ways to connect with people, but it must be done right.

Besides the obvious point of not making racial, sexual, or gender jokes, avoid "punching down." Never make a joke at someone else's expense in a professional setting, even if you know the person well.

I grew up with three brothers and about a half dozen boys our age on the block. The way we showed affection did not involve "I love you, man." No. We teased. If I tease you, it is a pretty good sign I like you and consider you part of my circle. This rarely looks good to others looking on, and I have been called out on it.

It is the same with sarcasm. A fine line exists between being perceived as witty and droll and being seen as flippant and unserious.

Self-deprecating humor, a joke at your own expense, is the best kind of humor. It makes you immediately accessible. Whenever I speak in public, I make some variation of a joke about my receding hairline and advancing waistline. Trite and silly? Of course, but the audience comes to my side right away every time.

You want to be seen as a serious person who does not take yourself too seriously. You're proud of your Stanford degree, and it is super impressive. I assure you, though, people don't want to hear about it more than once.

> When an influential person asks how you're doing, don't say "busy." Everyone is busy, and it sounds vaguely like a complaint. Rather, say, "Great, just left a meeting on the Sapphire Project, and I really think we're making progress." Be memorable.

We all have problems and stresses important to us yet oddly uninteresting to others, likely because they have problems and stresses of their own. Never assert your problems are more important than the problems of those around you.

If you have rank, don't "Bigfoot" people. I invoked my VP title under stress one day, and I still regret it. If you do this in front of peers, be prepared to lose standing in their eyes, because you will. Be as polite to the person filling your water glass at lunch as you are to your boss's boss.

Remember, you are trying to be memorable for the right reasons. You are trying to receive an invitation to a club—a club of executives.

People want pleasant people in their club.

# CHAPTER 4

# DEVELOPING SWAGGER

---

The dictionary relates the term "swagger" to a manner of walking with a confident gait. I want to look at this concept in a broader sense.

People who attract attention in an organization throw off a sense of "I got this." They are willing to take on the newest challenges. The bigger the spotlight, the better they perform. The ball goes to people like this when the game is on the line. At work, others seek them out for help because their advice carries a little more weight. We all know this hard-to-define quality.

Of course, the foundation of being admired for competence is being competent. You don't want a reputation as someone who uses razzle-dazzle to fake it. You'll be found out. A good place to start is to assess where you are in your career development from a technical standpoint.

Make sure you stay current with the latest certifications in your field. Some disciplines, like technology, move fast. Others, like human resources, move more slowly. I will touch on this more, but you need to accept the role of a lifelong learner in your profession.

It's important to become known as a person who can accomplish things. I recommend you do your best to make a fast start in any new organization. Go the extra mile when handed an assignment. Your fresh set of eyes will see things overlooked for a long time. Point those out in a diplomatic way, and make suggestions to resolve them. Make the people who hired you feel good about their decision. Their sponsorship is critical.

Once confident in your technical or business skills, focus on these strategies to show you are a person with potential.

## SHOW AMBITION

It is never wrong to make your ambitions known in your organization. This is a key reason some succeed and others don't. When an older or longer-tenured executive starts to think about succession, their minds will scan the environment for people who remind them of themselves earlier in their career. Similarity bias? If you have made your ambitions known to these people, your name goes to the front of the line. Do not make them guess.

The mere fact you express interest in taking on a bigger job demonstrates your innate confidence in your abilities. Confidence is an underpinning for swagger.

Things grow a bit dicey in this discussion because this is one of few areas in *Your Afternoon Mentor* where gender and ethnic differences come into play.

Women are overrepresented on college campuses and in professional schools—by a lot.

Yet men still control the law partnerships, the C-suites, and the board seats—by a lot.

I read an interesting article about why women do better in school and men do better at work.

Girls, generally, are more prone to be pleasers in school. They are more likely to sign up for honors classes and do extra credit work. They are more disposed to collaboration. They will polish their work to perfection because they tend to sharply focus on an A, because the A is an unmistakable sign people are pleased with you.

Boys, generally, are more content to put off studying until the last minute—I was guilty of this. In their minds, they can fake their way through the final—guilty again—and be thrilled with the B minus. Whew! They are more likely to compete with the other boys their age than collaborate. "Look at me!" comes the cry of the ambitious young boy on the playground. This evolves to "Hold my beer" in college. In their world, big, audacious displays of bravado in front of peers earn them status and identity. Who cares what the teachers think?

Why is this important?

Because girls become women who wait until things are perfect before they ask for the next job or the next raise, if they ever do.

Boys become men who will not hesitate to grab for the bigger opportunity, even if they think they are not quite ready. This makes sense, as they were not penalized for B-minus performance in the classroom and received status rewards for ballsy play from other boys growing up.

Many other factors explain the disparity between genders in professional life, not least of which is how motherhood disrupts career paths.

My experience supports this premise. It is well documented men more audaciously—there's that word again—market themselves, more aggressively negotiate their salaries at hire, and are more likely to ask for a raise. Women impose a form of tax on themselves for not doing this because employers often base a woman's new salary when hired or promoted, in part, on her current salary. I saw this over and over again in my career.

Studies also show women apologize more often in the workplace than men. This robs them of power. Of course, when you mess up, apologize. But don't say, "Sorry to bother you," when you could say, "May I have a moment of your time?" Absolutely do not apologize for asking an uncomfortable question or challenging a faulty assumption when working with others to solve a business problem. Also, an apology when giving critical feedback to a coworker or subordinate undercuts the message.

On many occasions, I've asked a female colleague why she was apologizing to me for something not meriting an apology. The question usually shocked her, and she rarely offered a good answer. I gently reminded her she was costing herself power.

Everyone should avoid these self-imposed restraints.

Also, without going too far down this path, some cultures and families reward conformity over individuality. In these groups, it may not be a good thing to try to stand out. If this is part of your background, you must deal with it somehow.

The bottom line is—in a Western-based organization—if you want to advance, tell someone.

## HAVE AN OPINION

Just as you should not be shy about expressing your ambition, you must develop the knack for expressing opinions on difficult, or even controversial, matters at work.

Remember, our whole goal is to earn you notice as someone with senior leadership potential. You will not impress anyone, or make yourself memorable in any way, if you expect to get along by going along. If you agree with everything, with everybody, every day, you will not stand out. You will exemplify conformity and fecklessness.

No doubt this can bring challenges. Especially if you are early- to midcareer and have yet to establish the gravitas naturally attached to age, experience, and rank. I remember this stage of my career clearly. The desire for acceptance as a team member, and to keep the paychecks coming, often forms a constant tension with the desire to make things better or help the organization avert pitfalls. I wish I could say I always had the courage to speak up. I know I didn't.

As an aside, you may one day have the misfortune of working with a dominant boss who takes everything personally or simply does not care what you have to say. You may find yourself at a place where dissent is actively discouraged. If either of these applies to you today, start looking for a new job tomorrow.

Consider how strong you are in the following three critical and interrelated skills, which will come up again later in our afternoon. They will help you become adept at holding your ground and sounding credible:

**Negotiating.** Develop the skill of obtaining what you want in a way that preserves relationships with, and the dignity of, others in your daily interactions. If you become good at this, others might not even know you are doing it.

**Influencing.** This is the art of winning people to your point of view, but it is not necessarily the same as negotiating. Become effective at influencing individuals and groups to follow your ideas.

**Conducting a critical conversation.** Read the seminal book written a few decades back called *Crucial Conversations*. You've probably already come across it if you have worked in an organization for any period of time. This book will help you stay within yourself when conducting high-stakes conversations.

A few more thoughts about sharing an opinion at work.

Remember, because you have an opinion does not mean everyone will be warm to it. Some losses will mix in with your wins. Avoid gloating when your idea carries the day, and take care to share credit.

More importantly, don't take a loss personally. Don't make excuses, and don't go up and down the hallway indicting the fools who disagreed with you. Once a decision has been made, your responsibility lies in helping to execute it. This, of course, assumes what you are being asked to do is legal, moral, ethical, and within policy. Avoid being seen as someone undermining a collective decision.


## CALMNESS IN THE STORM

Our final approach into Las Vegas took us over mountains on a hot summer afternoon. Our plane bounced all over the place, more than I had ever experienced. People around me were giving each other the side-eye to see if others were scared, too.

I had earned a pilot's license, and I knew we were flying through rising columns of warm air and sinking columns of cooling air—giant convections created by summer heat and made worse by mountains. Nevertheless, my fellow 140 passengers and I were genuinely concerned.

The pilot came on the intercom and, in the most calming and confident voice, said, "Ladies and gentlemen, we know this is uncomfortable. But it is August, and this is what happens in Las Vegas this time of year. We will be through this in about five minutes and have you at the gate in fifteen. So sit back, and relax. This will be over soon."

He sounded like he was pulling a canoe into the dock on a lazy Sunday afternoon.

Immediate relief settled throughout the cabin.

Swagger.

Being known as a person who can keep calm in turbulence will gain you instant trust and credibility.

Being known as someone who cannot handle pressure will stall your growth in your organization.

Here are some things to remember when the stress level spikes at work.

First, remember where you are. You are at work in a sales, technology, operational, or administrative job. Unless you sit in the cockpit of an airliner in severe turbulence, in the middle of a raging fire, or in an operating room performing brain surgery, lives and property are not at stake. What amped you up today will be an afterthought in a week. Keep perspective, always.

A term used in the mental-health field, "catastrophizing," describes when your mind takes over and predicts, even anticipates, the most negative outcome imaginable in a situation. If you find yourself in this trap often in your personal or professional life, seek assistance because you are making yourself and those around you miserable. The worst-case scenario, by definition, almost never comes to pass.

Remember you were hired for a reason. You would not be in the cockpit, in the burning building, or poking around inside somebody's brain if you had not already proven yourself capable of being there in the first place. Trust your instincts and training.

Develop the skill of breaking big problems into smaller ones, and go after those first. Often, a tricky situation resolves more quickly than expected when you start working on it. The key is to start. When your coworkers spin in circles, encourage them to stop by asking basic questions. "Where are we on this?" "What can we fix quickly?" "What is the worst that can happen?"

Walk away from a tough problem for a day or two. Regroup. Take a rest. Go outside. Practice yoga. Call a mentor for advice. Then revisit it. You'll be surprised at how often the answer lay right in front of you all along.

When in a tug-of-war with a no-win situation sapping your energy and ruining your sleep, drop your end of the rope. Drop it, and move on to the next thing on your plate.

Become known as a person who remains cool under pressure, and watch your role in an organization grow.


## GOOD JUDGMENT AND DECISION-MAKING

Related to the above, and as you will see later "this afternoon," people like working for good decision-makers. Leaders are more prone to entrust company resources, like their money and personnel, to people who show good judgment.

You can refine a skill you have used every day of your life as a sentient human being. As I've said several times now, so much of our behavior follows patterns, routines, and biases—and awareness of this helps us break through to something new.

This also applies to decision-making at work. Be deliberate in your approach when a significant decision puts you in the spotlight.

Others will see you as unsure of yourself—as a flip-flopper—if you unwind a decision made too quickly. They will think of you as indecisive if you avoid hard decisions because you are not comfortable, or even fearful. Both these behaviors make you look weak.

When making a significant decision at work,

**Clearly define the problem.** At a certain point, and after endless discussion, you must identify the root of an issue. You may be faced with a convoluted, tangled set of facts. Organize and reduce them to a simple problem statement, then test with others around you.

A Buddhist philosopher once said, "Some problems in life, you can control. Some problems in life, you cannot control. Therefore, you shouldn't have any problems."

Remember this at work and in life. Be discerning in what you can impact.

**Start the fact gathering.** Sounds logical, but don't forget our conversation about confirmation bias. It is easy to select the facts you want to lead you to the decision you already arrived at. Actively seek evidence contrary to your perspective before making the call.

When mediating between two people, do not make a decision until you hear from both sides.

**Consult the appropriate parties.** This is smart from a political and practical standpoint. You will want some cover for your decision when a lot is at stake. Attain this by involving key stakeholders early in the process. Make sure they do not fall into the similarity bias trap once you bring them in. Ask them to vet your thinking. Press them to serve as devil's advocates.

> We are all familiar with the Apollo 13 space mission that required the astronauts to abort the moon landing because of an explosion. Pull up the movie scene on YouTube where the flight director—Gene Kranz, played by Ed Harris—comes into a full conference room to gin up ideas on how to bring the crew home. He clearly defines the problem by drawing it on a blackboard, actively seeks input from others, keeps to the facts, and does not allow emotion to rule. Then, he decides whether his own intuition trusts the plan. It provides a great demonstration of how to make a tough decision when the stakes are high.
>
> Though neither you nor I will ever be in Kranz's position, nothing stops us from using his decision-making process.
>
> And nothing stops us from carrying a bit of his swagger.

**Anticipate all possible positive and negative outcomes.** List them, if possible.

**Realize sometimes you have only bad options.** Be prepared to choose the lesser of two evils instead of wishing for the landscape to change when you know, intuitively, it won't.

**Hold your decision to your nose.** How does it smell? Is the decision giving off an odor? If it is going against your intuition or prior experience, you may want to start the process again.

**Summarize and implement.** We've all left a meeting with unclear next steps. I always like to see people send a summary of proposed actions and assignments. Doing so makes you appear engaged and adds to the perception you are a person of substance.

Decision-making will come up again and again later in this book.

# CHAPTER 5

# AUTHENTICITY

When I set out to write *Your Afternoon Mentor*, I promised myself I'd avoid using inspirational quotes and HR buzzwords or otherwise sound like a yoga instructor—though I love yogi wisdom in measured doses. I wanted the book to sound real. To sound...well, authentic.

I will make an exception here because it's a good term to define the fourth critical element of executive presence: "authenticity." For me, authenticity describes a real person; someone who understands what they like and don't like, is true to self and values, and lives in the moment, with an awareness of how others in the world perceive them.

## KNOW YOURSELF

You've had some time to experiment in your work life if you are a midcareer professional. Maybe you've tried a few different roles in a couple of different fields, and you're looking for something that keeps you interested and plays to your strengths. Great; that is what you should be doing at this point in your working life.

There are many ways you can make this process more mindful. Available validated tools can help you understand your basic personality type, your likes and dislikes, and what motivates you.

One example is the DiSC personality test. This assessment will tell you the mix of dominance, influence, steadiness, and conscientiousness existing in your work mindset. It is sort of a DNA test for your professional personality.

Another example is the Myers-Briggs Type Indicator, commonly known as the MBTI. This instrument will help you understand if you are extroverted or introverted, describe how you receive information, explain the process your brain uses to make decisions, and determine the speed at which it does so.

Both of these assessments can be found online for free or for a nominal fee.

I am a big fan of these because once you understand who you are, you gain a better understanding of where you should be. When you are in the right job at the right place, your career takes on palpable momentum.

For example, I am not a detail person, and I don't like routine. I am more of a builder. I need to serve in a role where I create a new status quo, not as the caretaker of an old one. Understanding this helps me make critical career decisions. It also helps me decide where to put my focus at work and what kind of people I need around me to fill the gaps in my skillset.

The following shows some other ways of understanding who you are and how best to succeed at work.

If you are the person who naturally organizes your friends

in activities, this tells you something. If you mediate friction between friends and family, this tells you something, too. Think about what work and organizations you would pursue if you were an adventurer by nature. If you are creative, you will flail unless you can find an outlet for this energy.

Tell me where you spend your time, and I will tell you your passions.

So how do you spend your time?

Don't waste precious years of your career trying to figure out what grabs you at work and what makes your eyes glaze. The answers lie there for the taking; do a deep dive into your mind, interests, and behaviors, and the answers will come to you.

## FEEDBACK

A technically able person once worked for me. They were always there to answer any detailed questions, and they were almost always right. This person knew their stuff.

This person was also always in the middle of some kind of perceived drama and could not keep a team together. The most obvious faults, quite obvious, involved defensiveness and making excuses when things did not go well.

I sat them down and told them my own observations and feedback from others. I drew a picture of someone defensive and way too eager to blame others for their problems at work.

The person reacted to the feedback by becoming defensive and making excuses.

"Stop," I said. "Those things I suggested you not do? You're doing them right now."

More defensiveness.

Conversation cycle repeated.

Though I was giving this person the gift of feedback, they were too obtuse to open it. The person did not last long with me.

Two points about this anecdote.

First, feedback is at once all around you and difficult to find. People in your life and in your work environment respond to you in subtle ways. Maybe you are having a difficult time achieving positive outcomes at work or home. Or you could be struggling with relationships. Try to figure out what is causing the trouble and how you are contributing to it. Take the blinders off, and tease out what people and circumstances are trying to tell you.

If this does not work, ask for more direct feedback. At home, ask trusted people in your life if they observe behaviors limiting your success.

At work, ask your boss and peers how you are doing, what you are doing well, and where you need to improve. Ask for specific behaviors and examples. Let these folks know you are simply looking for ways to improve. Feedback is not easy for people to give, so keep pressing in a respectful way, and make it easy for them.

Don't wait to do this at performance-review time because the higher you go in an organization, the less likely you are to receive an evaluation. I recall two in my career. Many companies have dropped the annual review process altogether.

However, some organizations conduct a formal 360-degree feedback process, so volunteer to undergo this exercise if you can. It provides a great way to learn how others perceive you and your effectiveness.

When you receive the feedback, don't swat it back to the other person like you're returning a serve in a tennis match. Don't tell yourself stories about why the feedback is inaccurate. If you do, you are denying the same gift I was giving my former coworker. Open it, embrace it, and act on it.

I was quite driven early in my career. I once received feedback in a 360 review saying, "Kevin needs to put his finger away." Hmm. I took it as a sign I needed to turn the intensity level down a few notches when asking people to do something. To this day, years after I received that feedback, I have learned to slow things down when driver mode sets in. Nobody wants the boss wagging a finger in their face.

Ask and act.

## EMOTIONAL INTELLIGENCE

In 1995, the *New York Times* writer Daniel Goleman summarized and organized decades of research about how our feelings and emotions impact behavior. With it, he created a book called *Emotional Intelligence: Why It Can Matter More Than IQ.* Since then, so-called EQ has played a prominent role in leadership and executive development training and coaching.

Goleman and other psychologists posited our ability to perceive our environment and understand and manage our feelings and emotions in the environment can actually be more important than our raw intellectual horsepower.

For the purposes of our discussion about authenticity, let's briefly discuss the five elements of EQ, some of which I have already touched on. Give thought to how strong you are in each of these dimensions:

**Self-Awareness.** This refers to your ability to recognize your emotions as you are experiencing them.

We all react differently to stimuli in the environment. Some of us love change; others fear it. Some of us are quicker to anger and quicker to cool off. Something frustrating to me may barely be noticed by you. You can view a problem as an insurmountable mountain, where I see a pesky molehill. As we learned earlier, we can meet the same person and see vastly dissimilar people.

The self-aware person reflects on the source of their feelings in the moment. The more we understand what provokes our emotions, the better we can manage how our responses impact others. Giving your emotions primacy without this understanding will foreclose your ability to read how others are perceiving, or misperceiving, you in any given moment.

**Self-Regulation.** This speaks to how well you manage emotions as you feel them; it is the ability to steer yourself to a positive outcome, or at least avoid a negative one. Calmness in the storm.

Examples of poor self-regulation are abundant and easily recognizable. Lousy impulse control. Negative body language. Biting, sarcastic remarks about a person or situation. A defeatist attitude. Thinking rules don't apply to you. Pouting like a six-year-old denied a second bowl of Cocoa Puffs.

People with strong self-regulation skills think before they act. They keep their stress in check so they don't make a tough situation worse. They acknowledge the need to adapt on the fly when the circumstances demand flexibility. They humbly cede power, and may even shoulder undeserved blame, in service of a long-desired outcome. These folks know when to speak and are careful with the words they choose. More importantly, they know when to keep the yapper shut. They stay accountable to themselves and others.

The downsides to not managing your emotions will come up again later in this book.

**Motivation.** People with high emotional intelligence are driven to realize their full potential. They are grateful for the material rewards of success but are more interested in achievement and goal accomplishment. You need neither a carrot nor a stick to get them to move because they have abundant energy requiring an outlet. They are more optimistic than most and are consistently ambitious.

Other indicators of high motivation include intense intellectual curiosity, an openness to new people and ideas, and a general sense that the world is big, life is short, and opportunities are everywhere.

Executives I've met with this innate motivation are adept at inspiring others. They are also resilient when they encounter a setback. Again, more on this later.

**Empathy.** The first three elements of EQ describe how we encounter ourselves. Empathy describes how we encounter others.

Let's revisit our discussion of self-regard. We consider ourselves smarter than others, our ideas better, our problems more important, and our opinions more profound.

Having a high EQ requires you to set aside this and other biases and listen to—and seriously consider—the thoughts, opinions, experiences, and feeling of others. You must accept others perceive the world differently than you do, and their views merit the same consideration you give your own.

This is not difficult once you grant this notion currency. Your granddad told you to walk in another person's shoes before you judge them because he had accumulated a little wisdom. Pay attention to him.

If you cannot do this, you may plow forward into a situation where your goals and the goals of those around you are misaligned. Nobody wins in that situation.

> Have you ever sat behind home plate at a professional baseball game? It's not like watching from the outfield bleachers or the upper deck on the third baseline. The fastballs really zip, the breaking balls drop a foot right in front of the batter, and every fly ball starts off looking like a home run. It's the same game and action, except you perceive it differently. What you see really does depend on where you sit. Remember this when considering disparate points of view.

**Social Skills.** A lot of success in work and life comes down to how likable you are and how comfortable people are around you. We spoke to this a few minutes ago when discussing communication style. Be interested in others, and give them space to express themselves. Use a light touch, and treat everyone with respect, regardless of their status or what they can do for you.

Executives I've met with strong social skills create community and harmony. They excel at influencing and negotiating. They take care in being inclusive, avoiding favoritism, and slicing the pie so everyone gets a piece of resources or attention. They act quickly to mitigate conflict and are great coaches. Others look forward to seeing them in the day-to-day swim of the workplace.

I mostly buy into the concept of EQ, but I have to say I came across many people in business, and certain people in politics, who completely lacked EQ and still wound up going far.

Nevertheless, I found good takeaways from any book or article I read on the topic. I encourage you to learn more.

# CHAPTER 6

# NETWORKING

---

D og-ear this chapter.

Why? You will find no more important an activity to advance your career than networking.

I told you about the mentor who gently teased me for my worn-out pants. He also pointed me to three interesting and financially rewarding jobs. In fact, he was on the search committee for my penultimate job as the vice president of human resources at Arizona State University. He kept my résumé in play when others on the committee wanted to scrub me out because I did not have university experience. Notice this similarity bias at the organizational level. He did not work at the university but served on the committee because of his prominence in the community. He built an amazing network in Phoenix and the Southwest, and I benefitted from it.

Your network should be narrow and deep and broad and shallow at the same time.

When I say narrow and deep, I refer to the importance of knowing three to five people who can help you move your career. People like the person I mentioned. These folks must be heavy hitters in your company, your industry, or your community.

Senior-level, C-suite-type jobs are rarely posted publicly. Neither are seats on boards of directors advertised on Jobs.com or Craigslist. These jobs and seats become accessible only because one powerful person knows another powerful person looking for vetted, senior-level talent they can trust. Like it or not, an elite layer of leaders runs every industry or community. I do not ascribe nefarious motives to these people. On the contrary, they are the people who change things up; those who build things—the people who work to see the mayor elected.

Your job? Find these people, and cultivate a relationship with them.

Do this by employing all the tactics described so far. Be professional in your look and demeanor, call attention to yourself in a strategic way, and show swagger and authenticity when you come across them. Put your phone down in their presence, and introduce yourself on the elevator and at industry events. Make yourself memorable.

Another easy way to do this: ask them for help.

Our human nature finds it flattering when people approach us for wisdom or advice. I always encourage people in early- to midcareer to identify people higher in the pecking order for mentorship. This can be something as simple as a note telling someone you admire their accomplishments and how they carry themselves. Ask if you can set up a fifteen-minute call or meeting to introduce yourself. They will almost always accommodate you. They will also remember you if an opportunity arises.

I always say yes when someone more junior in HR asks for some time. I also always remember them, especially the students I am lucky enough to interact with. I never said no to any student interested in general career tips. We usually wind up as contacts on LinkedIn. I take delight in following their careers.

When your target network contact agrees to meet with you, come prepared with a brief elevator speech. Jot down three or four things you want them to know about you. Remember what I said about trying to wing it? Don't wing it in this meeting. Give a two-minute biography. Tell them about your near- and long-term goals. Search for the thing you have in common, and point it out. Then give a soft sell and clearly leave the impression you want to advance at work, in the community, and in life.

Let them do the majority of the talking. People like hearing their own voices. It's everyone's favorite sound in the world.

Don't put your contact on the spot by asking for a direct favor. Their to-do list is already full. Follow up with a simple thank you and a commitment to reciprocate if you are ever in a position to do so. This is all your target contact expects.

Continue to do the other things I talked about. Increase your visibility by taking on problems at work without being asked, accept speaking opportunities, and become active in industry and affinity groups. When you have enough heft on your résumé, seek opportunities on nonprofit boards. They are a great source of contacts because you meet people prominent in both their industries and their communities.

Let's talk about the broad and shallow network.

The standards for online networking include LinkedIn and other social media platforms. Such sites are less effective in growing one-to-one relationships. It is unlikely the CEO of a company will read your profile and make you a job offer. Yet who is to say some person in your contacts can't help you navigate to the same CEO?

I see LinkedIn and related sites as being more useful for sending broadcast messages. This is helpful in its own right. Have you ever noticed you ignore car ads on TV until you are thinking about buying a car? Then, every car ad catches your eye. Same concept. It won't hurt if people have at least a vague idea of who you are. It could trigger something in their brains if they ever want to reach out to you.

I read up on the publishing process when I decided to write this book. Sounded like a total hassle. You must develop a detailed proposal someone will actually look at, then you search for an agent who will take you on. Next, you scramble to find a publisher who thinks your book can sell 100,000 copies, which no book does unless the author is already famous. You have about a 5 percent chance of selling your book, even if it is good. After a year or so of this, you are back to where you started.

I did learn self-publishing and ebooks can be successful if you already have a broad set of contacts. Say hello to LinkedIn as a marketing channel.

Other opportunities include podcasts and webinars. A lot of companies use them for marketing and are always looking for guests. Many industry-specific websites are also looking for content. So consider writing quick-hit articles you can submit unsolicited. You will likely find some outlet to publish you. What a great way to position your name out there.

Think personal and powerful for in-person relationships. Think broadcast and social media for profile building.

Many online articles cover networking. They describe anything from the pedestrian, like where and how to wear your name badge at an industry event, to some of the richer concepts touched on here.

I said everything in this section of the book can be learned. Networking is no different.

## SUMMARY

In Part I, I discussed how people perceive you—and will promote or hire you—is based on how you look, how you communicate, how confident you appear, and how in-tune you are with yourself and others. I closed with a discussion about being a strong networker.

I bet you didn't hear anything you had not heard before. No surprise. My goal was to prompt you to ask yourself critical questions about how strong you show up in these areas. We can all improve, even if we sit at the top of our professions.

As a final exercise in Part I, write down two things you will do in each of these five areas to ready yourself for a promotion or a call from executive recruiters.

## Appearance

_____

_____

_____

Communication

_____

_____

_____


Swagger

_____

_____

_____


Authenticity

_____

_____

_____


Networking

_____

_____

_____

# PART II

# UNDERSTAND THE TRANSITION TO A SENIOR LEADERSHIP ROLE

At age thirty-five, I landed my first executive job at a newspaper holding company. I had a vice president's title, salary, office, and administrative assistant. My elation for jumping a level on the career ladder was tempered by a fair amount of stress and anxiety. I did not sleep much in the weeks leading up to my start date. I walked into my new office on my first day, saw the tenth-floor view of downtown Phoenix, took in the cherry paneling festooning the executive suite, and walked into the restroom to throw up.

This is not uncommon. I've heard similar stories from colleagues who have been stressed by the prospect of taking on new and bigger jobs. Few of us have so much confidence it pushes out all self-doubt.

Part of the uncertainty of taking on a bigger role is not knowing the basics of a strategic leadership job. This is something rarely taught in business school. Even if it were, many leaders did not go to business school. Most people go through an entire career without ever learning fundamental, effective senior-leadership skills.

There is also a phenomenon known as "imposter syndrome," a collection of feelings of inadequacy, like you don't really belong in your job and are pulling off a fraud on those around you. Though women and minorities are believed to be more susceptible to imposter syndrome, everyone encounters this as at some point in their career.

I will help you through this anxiety in this section of *Your Afternoon Mentor* by talking about the difference between being promoted and being hired into a senior job. Then I will shift to discuss making the transition from the comfortable tactical work to the less-comfortable strategic responsibility. I'm going to ask you to identify what works for you in leadership and what does not. You'll be offered my time-tested observations on the five key, critical executive skills.

# CHAPTER 7

# THE PATHWAYS TO A SENIOR LEADERSHIP JOB

---

We'll spend time later talking about the importance of actively managing your career over the long haul. You'll see how networking, preparation, good judgment, reputation, and luck congeal to form a lubricant that keeps the gears of your career meshing smoothly.

Your first few senior-level jobs will be the most difficult to land because, as we've seen, somebody somewhere needs to trust you can leap the chasm to a much bigger job. The good news is after you've proven yourself a bit, jobs look for you instead of the other way around.

Every executive's journey will look radically different, but they all start with the first step. As you start yours, understand the two major pathways to a senior role.

## PROMOTED INTO A SENIOR LEADERSHIP POSITION

Many companies prefer to promote from within for these reasons:

**Continuity of operations.** Smart companies do this by building a strong succession plan to mitigate any disruption or risk a senior leadership change might cause. If things are humming along in an organization, and it does a good job of developing people, it'll take this path.

**Known commodity.** Companies that do a good job evaluating internal candidates know their strengths and weakness. A more informed decision about someone's leadership abilities reduces the chance of a skill or culture mismatch.

**Talent retention.** Finding and grooming employees with leadership potential is a time-consuming, expensive exercise. Retaining employees who have many career options creates a challenge in a competitive talent market—and the market for talent is always tight and recession proof. Strong employees will leave if they don't see a career path forward in their current company.

Good on you if you work for a company that hires, retains, develops, and promotes leaders internally.

The downsides to taking an internal promotion are few, but they should be noted.

First, you will likely be managing former peers. This can be challenging, and I will talk more about it later.

The decision to wait for a promotion or seek options elsewhere will depend on where you sit on your career arc, your long-term goals, and your personal situation at the moment. You may be giving your own development short shrift by not making a strategic career move outside your organization when a window opens. Expect a burst of career creative energy and renewal when you change organizations and industries. These changes will make your life more interesting and you better at what you do. I'll revisit this too.


## HIRED INTO A SENIOR LEADERSHIP POSITION

Companies go outside the organization for an executive hire for these reasons:

**An organization is broken.** It is not uncommon to see an organization, or functions within an organization, run aground by an incompetent or corrupt leader. In this case, a board or executive team may think it has no choice but to bring in someone new, despite having internal candidates who can step up.

As an aside: if your former boss left under a cloud, or if your department is seen as an underperformer, accept the possibility the taint may have rubbed off on you. Polish the résumé.

**An organization needs new energy.** Things may not be broken, but there may be a perception they need fixing anyway. Companies often think the best way to shake things up is to look outside themselves. I've been in on this conversation many times. The hiring decision-makers may see internal options and say, "Meh." They start looking for the elusive person who checks every box on the wish list.

Remember confirmation bias? Once the decision to go outside is made, the organization plows through, if for no other reason than to justify its own decision, even if the external candidates are not demonstrably stronger than internal options.

**Succession.** Sometimes, a forward-looking senior leader looks around for her successor and does not see one. An external hire is the only viable route.

Congratulations if you've been hired to fix what has been damaged, energize a slothful organization, or be groomed for bigger things. You'll gain financial reward and have a great chance to grow and make your mark.

Your path could be fraught with landmines, however.

Most studies show external hires fail at a higher rate than internal promotions. The most common reasons are:

- It takes an external hire longer than anticipated to come up to speed with the new organization's operations.

- External hires have a difficult time adapting to the new employer's culture.

- The new executive makes decisions too quickly.

- The new executive makes decisions too slowly.

- Expectations of both the employer and new executive are too unrealistic.

- External hires often must overcome resentment from people who have been passed over. Going outside sends a signal to the internal pool the organization sees them as limited in potential. Nobody likes this message.

- A new leader's family may not adapt well to a new city or lifestyle.

Cultivate relationships with executive recruiters. Respond to them, even if you're not the right person for the role they're recruiting. Tell them why you're not interested and ask them to ping you if something closer to your needs or experience comes their way. Timing is everything in a career move. They may have an assignment perfect for you next month or next year, and you'll be the first person they call.

I could go on here. The point is, you can be successful in this scenario, and you can leverage your success into an even bigger opportunity. You must be smart and self-aware. The skills I have addressed, and will discuss shortly, will help you through this.

# CHAPTER 8

# LEADERSHIP TRANSITIONS

Take a look at this chart.

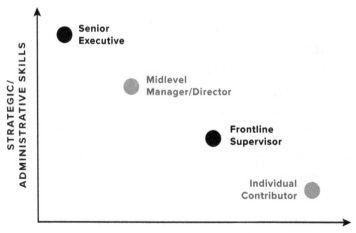

**Leadership Transitions**

The horizontal axis plots tactical and technical skills, and the vertical axis plots strategic and administrative skills.

Jobs requiring high technical skill but with low strategic impact are usually multi-incumbent, meaning many people do the same type of job. The work can be somewhat repetitive, and the people who staff them have less discretion over how they complete their tasks. This can be true even for people with remarkable skills: an airline pilot or nuclear control-room operator.

Staff in these roles have less interaction with other departments, fewer constituencies to keep happy, and fewer projects to juggle. Sometimes, others refer to them as "individual contributors," and they can often labor under many levels of management.

Organizations and economies do not work without these jobs.

For many, the first step into leadership is as a front-line supervisor. This may be one of the most challenging roles in an organization. People are often tapped for a supervisor job because they demonstrate high mastery and productivity as an individual contributor. The best engineer becomes lead engineer; the strongest salesperson becomes sales manager.

Yet the organization rarely makes an effort to ascertain if a person has basic leadership ability before promoting them. We will shortly see leadership is a collection of behaviors, skills, and attitudes. Many companies don't offer even rudimentary supervisory training in these areas, or they make it optional. There's the leadership whirlpool. Jump in. Hope you can swim.

Some employees accept the front-line supervisor job because it comes with a larger paycheck, while others accept due to societal pressure to advance or the desire to make their parents and partner proud. Some feel they simply can't say no. They never stop to ask themselves if they really want the job. This is why we spent time talking about self-knowledge in Part I.

However, many more employees take the role because they are fulfilled by the challenge, enjoy working with people, and see it as a way to have more influence over their own workday.

Go back to the chart. Front-line supervisors are asked to execute the company's strategic mission and objectives, even though they likely had little input into their development. They translate communication and decisions from the hierarchy but have to finesse feedback they send back up the chain, lest they be seen as second-guessers or complainers from the egos on the higher floors. They have to stretch resources in tough times, as most companies cut the front-line staff in a downturn because we all know the C-suite people are too valuable to let go. A person who can do all this well should be commended, retained, and developed.

Front-line supervisors have always been my favorite people wherever I've worked. The ones who are suited to the role and are starting out are usually very enthusiastic and want to improve. They are genuinely grateful when given training, guidance, and mentorship.

Those who have been in the role a while, the grizzled veterans, usually have an amusing and harmless cynical streak, and you can learn a heck of lot if you ask them what's happening in the real world. They've survived many regime changes and flavor-of-the-month programs, and they show up every day to get the job done. They are a great source of organizational history and institutional knowledge.

> Every organization has politics—not because they are
> good or bad, but because they are organizations. They
> can be small riffles on the water in one place and Class
> IV rapids in another. Every boatman will tell you to meet
> the waves head on. There are plenty of articles and books
> on navigating politics, so learn more. Remember the im-
> portance of authenticity, networking, and relationships.
> Over time, you'll develop a feel for the currents.

We transition now to the realm of the senior leader in our discussion of the mid-level manager/director job.

Here, leaders are drifting further away from the individual contributors on the "shop floor" and more removed from the customer. Directors should spend at least half their time shaping and refining the divisions they run, exploring new business opportunities, and working on longer-term projects. Anything less demonstrates a fundamental misunderstanding of the role.

One assumes directors have mastered the basics of leading people, but we know this is not always the case. Nevertheless, they are now leading leaders instead of first-line employees. This presents its own challenges, as their direct reports are settled into their supervisory roles and have strong opinions about how things should be. Directors are the arbiters of how resources in their units are distributed and the mediators of tougher personnel decisions. The solutions to these problems are rarely clear cut. Every organization needs to calm this internal jostling to excel, and a different approach to managing people is called for.

Directors work across units, functions, and geography. The ability to communicate, influence, and negotiate is much more important than any technical skill they may have. Their profile is rising with both those above and below them on the org chart. Their names are out there in the ether, and people they don't know are defining them based on scraps of gossip picked up in the hallway.

The pyramid in a hierarchal organization is coming to a point; top jobs in flat organizations are rarer by design. Directors are now competing with some very sharp people to move up to a limited number of opportunities. The criteria for promotion are now more esoteric, the final decision more subjective.

Remember our discussion of executive presence? You better believe the CEO is asking about yours.

Vice president-level leaders have near-zero reliance on the technical. Almost everything about the job comes down to strategic and communication skills.

They usually embody single-incumbent roles. You rarely see two vice presidents running the same function. Like directors, these people must work across departments. You can now add outside audiences to the mix. Board members, investors, analysts, customers, competitors, and sometimes news reporters are assessing the company or organization by examining them. People not only watch the members of an executive team, they dissect their moves and motives.

They control the rudder and throttle of their organizations. They make the multimillion-dollar decision about where to build the next production plant, then wear a goofy hard hat at the groundbreaking ceremony. They decide which markets to enter or exit. Vice presidents usually have stock options or shares, so they pay very close attention to the financials. They represent the organization at the annual Heart Ball. Sometimes, they're invited to drop wisdom into the 6:00 a.m. time slot on a business news channel.

In these high-visibility roles, success and failure live right there in full view. Now, more than ever, a premium is placed on the softer skills, an accessible persona, and an inclusive worldview.

A strategic job is difficult to obtain and, when lost, difficult to replace.

The long-term success of an organization, sometimes an industry or community, rides on the abilities of the people in these jobs. The people who are really good at them rightly take their place in the pantheon of their company's history.

The transition from the lower-right to the upper-left in the chart is rarely crisp because of the difference in skills required. You can't walk into a class as a tactical thinker and emerge three hours later as a strategic thinker. Meaningful experience is needed. This explains why when you graduate from Annapolis, they present you with an ensign's bar, not an admiral's star.

Many people already in "strategic" jobs complain they are still simply putting out fires all day, only the fires are a lot bigger. Still others secretly say they have no idea what being strategic even means.

Being strategic—being an executive—is a mindset. A way of looking objectively at your role and what it entails. Though some will be more comfortable thinking strategically than others, everyone can improve. While you may not yet have the experience, there are five critical strategic skills you can easily understand and develop.

First, though, I'm going to take you on a brief detour.

# CHAPTER 9

# EFFECTIVE LEADERSHIP BEHAVIORS

―――――――――
―――――――――

Here, I define the difference between a skill and a behavior. They can interact and complement each other, but they are not the same.

A skill is the ability to do something well, a level of expertise. It can be something raw, ragged, under constant refinement, and randomly successful, like my golf swing. Or it can be exquisitely honed, like B. B. King's blues guitar playing. A skill can be developed, even mastered, with enough focus and practice.

A behavior is an aspect of the way we conduct ourselves, the things we do on a frequent basis. All of us default to certain behaviors: some welcomed by others, some not so much. A behavior can be changed if one is aware of it and decides to make corrections in the moment.

Time for an exercise.

Think of a poor leader you've known, and list five to seven ineffective behaviors they displayed:

_____

_____

_____

_____

_____

_____

Now, think of good leader you've known, and list five to seven effective behaviors they displayed:

_____

_____

_____

_____

_____

_____

I'm confident we will soon discuss most, if not all, the behaviors you wrote down. This is because they are so common we can all identify them without too much thought. People give me virtually the same list whenever I ask this question.

You would think because they are so familiar leaders in organizations would have quit the ineffective and latched onto the effective behaviors.

You would be wrong.

Even the best leaders do ineffective things, but they make course corrections when they find themselves doing them.

Remember me catching myself now, before wagging my finger? Remember self-awareness?

Let's go deep into a few of these so you can do the same.

## INEFFECTIVE CHARACTERISTICS

**Micromanage.** People do not like their bosses to micromanage and viscerally rebel against it. Micromanagers have a hard time letting go of the tactical. People often micromanage because they emerged from an individual-contributor role and miss the familiar things they used to do well or don't know where to spend their time. This is a common trap for those promoted from within and front-line supervisors.

A micromanager will check in with you frequently and second-guess your approach to your own task. They give you a project, tell you it's yours to do, then quickly correct you when you wander from the path they decided you should take. These people come off as extremely insecure. Praise rarely comes from a micromanager, but minor criticism flows like a bitter India pale ale from a beer tap.

Good luck giving feedback to a micromanager. They will tell you what you did wrong in the conversation and why you should have done it their way.

**Intimidate/Bully.** People often tell their HR person, "My boss yelled at me." It happens sometimes, for sure. However, I see this as shorthand to describe generally abusive behavior. It's more likely the person "yelling" makes them miserable in other, less-obvious ways.

Bullies like to remind people they are in control—always. They demean people in private and in public, often through words or a nonverbal gesture, like a sigh or an eye roll. An intimidating boss couches pointed barbs as a joke, then tells you you're too sensitive. These people don't know the difference between criticism as coaching and criticism as destruction.

They like to pit you against another person and go to the other person to pit them against you. You'll have to guess what you did to upset them because they give you the silent treatment to show you their displeasure. Bullies allow factions to form in the workplace and don't care if they show favoritism to the sycophants on the team.

Good luck giving this person feedback. You will make an enemy for life.

People take a deep and deserved sigh of relief when freed from this boss. Karma, however, is not far over the horizon. You rarely see bullies last in leadership over the long haul.

**Self-Absorption.** This leader may not have a mean streak, but they can still act as a jerk. They like to preen and hog the spotlight. Status means a lot to them, and they believe themselves indispensable. The self-absorbed claim credit for the work of others because they honestly think they did it themselves. They take a slide deck you worked on for weeks and slap their name on it before it goes to the CEO.

They shed blame because they cannot fathom anyone as brilliant as they are can make a mistake. Your advice bounces right off their forehead because who are you to give advice? Your reluctance to embrace their ideas showcases another example of your inherent and unspoken inferiority.

The self-absorbed leader is obsequious when walking the CEO through your department but won't introduce you even if you're standing three feet away. He sets rules for the team he won't follow himself. When work needs doing on a Saturday, expect to see everyone at the office except him because he had a tee time he could not change. When he sees you on Monday, he'll brag he shot a seventy-nine and won't even ask about the project you worked on all weekend.

He flirts with your wife at company events. Did he mention he shot a seventy-nine last weekend? He is the first person in line when lunch is brought in and will elbow you out of the way during a fire drill.

Good luck giving advice to the self-absorbed leader. They are too busy admiring themselves in the mirror.

**Poor listening.** We all want to perform at work, and we like a measure of independence. We also expect the boss to pay attention to the things we do and respond when we need help. It's frustrating to need to reeducate the boss on things discussed several times prior. When an issue we warned about blows up, or a deadline is busted despite our best efforts, we have to find a clever and career-preserving way of saying, "Boss, I told you so."

Poor listening manifests in a physical way. You are interacting with your supervisor while she reads through her email or scrolls through her phone. Maybe you think you have your boss's attention, but she is too busy framing her response to you in her mind while you're speaking. You can see you're being ignored. At some point, she loses all interest in you and doesn't even try to hide it. You walk out of her office with only half the things on your list addressed.

Good luck giving feedback to a poor listener. Well…they don't listen.

**Invisibility.** An invisible leader is simply not there physically or mentally. These folks may be bored, burnt out, retired in place, or looking for another job. Invisible leaders captain drifting ships. Employees need and want direction when things go well, and more so when things come off the rails.

Your emails to this person pile up, and you must now yap like a hungry terrier to move things. Information dribbles to employees with an invisible leader like the last ounce of ketchup from the jar. Better be plugged into the grapevine so you'll know what's going on in the company.

Projects don't launch or end. You and your coworkers miss out on your share of company resources. The invisible leader gives everyone the same merit increase, so the incentive to perform evaporates. Employees who work for an invisible leader quickly disengage from the company's mission. If he does not care, why should they?

Good luck asking these people for even a grain of guidance. You won't be able to find them.

**Indecisiveness.** An indecisive leader waits for perfect conditions before they move—and things will never be perfect. She wants more data, even if the data is of marginal value and not material to the decision. Continuity and accomplishment wane as priorities constantly shift. The indecision leads to missed opportunities for the organization and the people who work for it.

Issues go around in circles, like planes waiting for clearance to land. Did you develop a great plan to solve a big problem or roll out a new program or product? You'll scramble at the last minute with an indecisive leader, and the results you hoped for will fall short of your standards. The last person to talk to an indecisive leader on a controversial topic often has the most influence.

Weak performers love indecisive leaders because they let them take advantage. Strong performers move on.

Good luck with an indecisive leader. You're going to have a constant ache from beating your head against a wall.

## THE EFFECTIVE

And now for the positive characteristics of a leader. Commit these to memory.

**Delegation.** A good leader delegates. As a delegator, you focus more on outcomes than processes, more on achievement than activity. You understand doing something differently is not the same as doing something wrong. Good delegators develop an intuition for who on the team can be trusted to do what and when. You set up clear checkpoints on a project or task and let your team go.

Think about how energizing it is when your boss gives you a meaty task or assignment—it is so gratifying to know you have been trusted to deliver for her or for your team. Being given room to run and be creative is one of the most inherently rewarding aspects of going to work.

**Active listening.** Your attention serves as the most important thing you offer as a leader. Create a listening environment by removing distractions and physically demonstrating your presence in the moment. Turn away from your computer and rotate your phone upside down when speaking with someone. By the way, you're fooling no one when surfing the internet while on a Zoom or conference call.

Don't offer an opinion too early in the conversation because you tilt the outcome. Ask open-ended questions. Reframe what you heard. Summarize the conversation when done to avoid confusion about next steps.

Walking away from a productive conversation with the boss is stimulating. Solving a problem or coming up with cool new ideas collaboratively validates one's status in the organization. Attention is an unmistakable sign of respect.

**Follow-Through.** Be selective about what you agree to do and when you agree to do it because you create a contract. People lose faith and will no longer do business with a person who breaks a contract. Make a daily list of your commitments, and do the most difficult thing first. Meet head-on any failure to deliver on a promise, and don't obfuscate or create false hope.

Working with someone who follows through strengthens the bonds of partnership and builds trust. Having an implicit understanding of "If I deliver for you, you will deliver for me" creates a sense of momentum.

**Decisiveness.** I have hit on this point a couple of times now. To refresh, develop a decision-making process you find works for you. Don't leap, but don't delay. Collect all pertinent information, engage all appropriate audiences, and screen the decision against your experience and intuition; then go.

Decisiveness eliminates ambiguity and promotes productivity. The energy saved from rehashing the same topic or regaining a consensus can be put against the task at hand.

**Consistency.** Be the same person every day. Don't make your people guess your mood. Use your knowledge of self-awareness and emotional intelligence to understand how your emotions in the moment influence your behavior and affect those around you. Separate your work challenges from your personal challenges. You will have favorite employees, but you cannot show favoritism. Find a predictable and effective, but not inflexible, approach to your work, and settle on it.

Consistency improves other aspects of life. You will not achieve any business or personal goal without consistency. You won't be in great physical shape working out sporadically. No—the only way to achieve your goals is to methodically persist. Plus, your friends and family will love you all the more if they know they can rely on you.

**Recognition.** Pay and benefits are a critical part of the work contract. Yet it's interesting how rarely we think about them. Studies show they quickly lose their power to motivate. It's doubtful you think about your paycheck on the way to work or during crunch time on a project. We usually do our best work when committed to a place where we feel valued.

Think back to a time you received praise for a job well done. It felt so good you easily remembered it. You just proved how powerful recognition can be. A good leader knows when and how to call out good performance.

**Visibility.** Keeping up with your email, while admirable, is not leadership. Be visible to all the areas you lead. People who work for you can be tentative about entering your office domain, so relieve them of this stress by going to theirs. Vary the locations of your standing meetings. Walk through the office to be social and to simply say hello. Make eye contact. Use the humor strategies we discussed to keep things light.

A boss in a good mood and genuinely interested in people turns the workplace into a community.

A couple of points before we move on from the topic of leadership behaviors.

First, go back to what you wrote in the exercise at the beginning of this chapter and come up with a few examples in your own mind for every behavior we did not discuss.

I doubt you had much trouble because, as noted, the behaviors are so universal we experience them from leaders every day. These behaviors were effective, or not, fifty years ago, and they will be effective, or not, fifty years from now.

> People generally don't leave companies; they leave bosses. Look back to your own experience. If you were ever unhappy at work, the source of your discontent was likely your boss. If you can't keep a team together and can't figure out why, take a quick look in the mirror. Adjust your approach to people.

Don't let the topic of leadership intimidate you. Most of the thousands of leadership books you won't read, or the dozens of webinars you won't pay attention to, refer to these behaviors in one way or another. No need to thank me for saving you so much time and money.

Second, to emphasize, even the most-effective leaders demonstrate ineffective behaviors at times. If you asked anyone who ever worked for me, they would tell you, eagerly, I did not always listen or follow through on something. I admit it. I'm human. But I do know what works. My challenge, and yours, is to minimize the ineffective behaviors and maximize the positive. You can do this only if you are alert to both.

# CHAPTER 10

# FIVE CRITICAL AND STRATEGIC EXECUTIVE SKILLS

---

This chapter is the heart of Part II—understanding the transition to a senior leadership role. You must develop five skills if you hope to succeed as an executive. All can be learned and emulated. I again refer you to your own experience with great leaders you've met at work or in your community.

## SKILL ONE: SETTING OUT A CLEAR VISION

Arizona State University was a second-tier state school when I went there for my undergraduate degree during the dying days of disco.

Mostly commuter, there were no distinguished programs besides a football team dominating its conference. Sponsored research, a key quality metric for any university, ranked near zero. As did its endowment. The faculty and student body lacked diversity.

If you needed Econ 420 to graduate and it was not offered this semester, you waited for next semester. The only time the school ever touched you—ever made it feel as if it knew you were alive—was if you missed paying a parking ticket. Graduation and retention rates were not great. A lot of students left and never came back because of the uncaring, unfocused culture. This was true even when I went back for an MBA in the early nineties.

I never apologized for my degrees from ASU, but they did not make the résumé sizzle, either.

In 2002, Michael Crow showed up to take the reins as president. He laid out the basics of the following charter in his inaugural address.

"ASU is a comprehensive public research university, measured not by whom we exclude, but rather by whom we include and how they succeed; advancing research and discovery of public value; and assuming fundamental responsibility for the economic, social, cultural and overall health of the communities it serves."

By 2021, ASU enrolled 130,000 students from more than 140 countries and all fifty states. All major programs ranked in the top twenty-five; most reached the top ten. Young people who had their choice of schools came to the university. The faculty better represented society as a whole and received many accolades for quality.

First-generation college students comprised about a third of the student body and reflected the racial, ethnic, and economic diversity in Arizona. Yet graduation rates approached those of the most selective public schools, like the University of Michigan or UT Austin. ASU began to lead the nation in the production of Fulbright Scholars and National Hispanic Scholars. It shipped more graduates to Silicon Valley than any school in California. Every blue-chip company sent recruiters.

Annual research funding exceeded $650 million, which put it in the top ten of all universities without a medical school. The endowment blew past $1 billion and outpaced growth for comparable schools. ASU is now ranked consistently as part of the top 1 percent of universities in the world.

A commercial for ASU? Absolutely. I am proud of what we accomplished and privileged to have played a part in it. If you or your kids want a great educational experience in a large, diverse, public research school, go to ASU.

Here is my point.

The charter contains forty-seven words.

The reason ASU stacked up so much success is because Crow never wavered from the vision he had for the school. He may have added a word here, deleted a word there, but the essence of the charter did not change.

He excelled at keeping students, the leadership team, faculty, and staff focused on the charter. He used the charter to screen every investment made in people, programs, or physical plant. Did the investment promote quality, inclusion, and access? Did it support the research enterprise? Did it help fulfill the school's responsibilities to the community?

If you want this level of success, you must lay out a vision, a charter, for your own organization.

Ask yourself a few basic questions, and answer them in language a sixth grader can understand.

Who do we want to be?

What do we want to do?

How do we want to do it?

How can we leave things better than we found them?

I said in the Introduction of this book I wanted to target my message to early- to midcareer types with the desire to move up. I opted to use clear language and avoid aspirational clichés and confusing diagrams. I promised not to go too deep into any one topic area. Stories would be used to keep from boring you to death. I created my own form of a charter, and it kept me disciplined whenever I sat down to write.

Apply the same rigor when you enter a new senior leadership role. Think clearly about the outcomes you seek, and work backward from them.

When this is all settled, make short-, mid-, and long-term plans. Don't go out more than three years because things change too fast. Be tactical and realistic about what you can do over the next twelve, eighteen, or thirty-six months.

Drill yourself and your team with these questions:

- Does the organization support our charter?

- Do we have the staff to execute?

- Is there a reward structure in place to promote success?

- Will finances and systems be sufficient?

This is a critical exercise because if you answer no to any of these, your plans will not be realized, and support for your vision and charter will unravel. Or your vision will simply be forgotten.

You must then communicate your vision and plans in your own voice.

Then, communicate them again in your own voice—every time you have the chance.

Be boring and relentless in how you communicate your vision and plans.

I became so familiar with the ASU charter I could calmly recite it word by word if I were ever held at gunpoint and told my life depended on it. Not because Michael Crow lacked imagination and could not come up with a new riff. Instead, he communicated his vision in almost every faculty, staff, or student forum I saw him conduct. He said it to parents, alumni, the regents, the legislature, the governor, and the local and national media. He said it in front of think tanks and potential donors. Not in a dry and rote way; he did not actually recite it. But he always made some reference to the charter to set context for his remarks on the topic of the day.

Increase your chance for success as an executive by developing a vision easily conveyed to a variety of audiences.

## SKILL TWO: BUILDING A TEAM

How do you assemble a competitive baseball or softball team?

Start with a solid catcher. They must be tough because this is the most taxing mental and physical position on the field. The catcher must be able to manage the pitcher, the umpire, and the strategy on defense. A strong arm is a must to prevent base runners from stealing second or third. It helps if they can hit, though it's not critical. If they do all the other things well, they will prevent many more runs than they create.

First and third basemen possess exceedingly quick gloves because balls come at them so fast. Third base needs fielding range and the strongest arm of any infielder. A player with a great glove but less range and a weaker arm is better suited for first base. Both must hit, preferably for power.

The most agile players on the diamond will be the shortstop and second baseman because they cover a lot of ground to both the right and the left. They play a role in almost every double play, so they need a high level of athleticism. Most likely the smallest players on the field, their batting and power averages trend lower, so the team gains a huge bonus when these players can hit.

All outfielders must be able to hit for average and power. The fastest player goes in center to cover the vastest part of the field. Your right fielder needs a cannon for an arm because the throw from deep right to third base is the toughest in the game and saves runs. The left fielder is least athletic because they cover less ground and mostly make throws to second base or the cutoff man.

You then collect a cadre of both left- and right-handed starting pitchers who can throw quality pitches for at least five innings. You need another four or five relievers who can keep the ball in the ballpark until they hand it over to the closer in the last inning.

I think you understand. A strong team embodies people with different skills matched to a position.

Your first job as a new coach is to assess the talent you currently employ and the talent you need for the different positions on the team.

Sounds easy, right? Yet most failed leaders will admit they took too long to put their team in place or weed out those who could not play.

It can be a heck of a lot of fun if you do it right. Serving as the conductor, the coach, of a group of smart and good-humored people is extremely satisfying. The workplace crackles when the chemistry is right, and successes start to come because everyone—everyone—likes to play on a winning team.

A caution: remove your biases when drafting your team.

I found someone who appeared to me the perfect candidate for a job I was having a hard time filling. He showed up to meet me well dressed and prepared. I liked him right away. I was rooting so hard for him during the interview I actually steered his answers on more than a few questions.

I was clear with him about what the job paid and what resources he would have to work with. He pressed through negotiations, and I went further than I wanted to with a starting salary. This created an internal inequity and would ultimately lead to bad feelings with the rest of my team.

He asked for more staff in one of our last conversations before he accepted, which was not possible. He asked for a bigger title, and I told him I could not do it because I would have to reopen the search. My antennae were up, signals were being sent, but I really wanted him to fill the job.

Things did not change when he started. He asked again for the things I told him he could not have within a few days of arrival. He took a dislike to the location of his office and made a few negative comments about having to pay for parking. It became apparent he was more interested in the trappings of the job than the job itself.

Others noticed and made sure I knew they noticed. Every one of our update meetings ended with a request for more this or more that, and I started to dread them. We never quite meshed, and our short and contentious work relationship made us both unhappy. I was relieved when he left.

I fell victim to confirmation bias throughout the hiring process as I latched onto the things I liked about him and ignored the things—the flashing red lights—that made me less sure.

When you hire, you will be inclined to look closer at people who are like you or came from your alma mater or former company because humans have similarity bias, and you are human. There is nothing inherently wrong with this, but don't do it to the point where you exclude others.

Does a financial or technology candidate honestly need direct industry experience? Does a person truly need a master's degree for consideration? What difference does ten years' experience make versus five? Do you have an implicit bias for these attributes? You are overlooking great talent if you focus on criteria of dubious relevance.

Be intentional about creating diversity in all its forms on your leadership team. Not because it is a nice thing to do but because it is a critical thing to do. You don't have to do it all at once, but always be thinking about your current team's skill mix and your plan to fill any gaps. This is one form of networking. Be on the lookout for talent in your travels inside and outside your organization. Take pride in mining and polishing rough diamonds.

Coach your team once it's put together. Do this by developing the skill of giving feedback. This can be done formally, per your company's performance-management system—we all know how great they are. I prefer you do it informally and often. Coaching opportunities abound, so take advantage of them. This is one of those areas where you must become proficient. Do more research.

I'm going to take a slightly negative jog here. Coaching is the most important thing you can do, but you will have a limited budget of time and energy to do it. Spend the majority of your resources making your good players even better.

Then be impatient with your weaker players.

Poor performance is thought of as an issue of skill, but I see it as a matter of will. Will the members of your team be supportive, or will they be secretly resistant? Will they bring positive energy and a sense of optimism, or will they need dragging along when you take them in a new direction? Will they respond to your constructive criticisms, or will they stubbornly refuse to change? Will they effectively dare you to deal with their toxicity?

If, through coaching, you've set out reasonable, equitable expectations and a player does not respond, cut them from the team. Cut them like a football coach releases a player who shows up out of shape and without having read the playbook. Your chances of turning this person around are next to nothing. In the meantime, your star players, the ones to whom you should devote your time and energy, are rolling their eyes in frustration.

Don't let the HR geeks or the employment attorneys scare you. If your company has a formal discipline process, follow it, but be aggressive. I have been involved in dozens of terminations involving people like this, and I have never been successfully sued. Not once. If you need to use a severance package in exchange for a signature on a release, consider it a cost of doing business.

I cannot emphasize this enough. Your job is to create an environment where strong performers thrive and weak attitudes are not tolerated.

One final point on team building and coaching.

Make every team member who is interested and capable ready for the next job. You must prepare them for bigger and better roles, either inside or outside the company. An executive known as a people-developer attracts even more talent.

Building and coaching a team is the most emotionally fulfilling thing you do when you enter a senior leadership role.

## SKILL THREE:
## BE DELIBERATE ABOUT BUILDING A CULTURE

In 2008, two young men named Travis Kalanick and Garrett Camp attended a tech conference in Paris and could not find a cab during a snowstorm. They thought of an idea: a limousine-sharing company where reservations could be made using a smartphone.

Thus, Uber was born.

Both were already rich, having sold startup software companies for millions. They let themselves marinate in the idea for a year or so. When they joined forces again to build the concept into a company, Kalanick emerged as the "idea incubator" between the two. From then on, he cemented his reputation as a win-at-all-cost type who thought rules applied to others.

This reputation did not improve as the company grew. He wound up in public tussles with other tech giants, like Apple. Uber became known for trying creative ways to bypass local transportation regulations in the markets it entered. It often found itself in high-profile legal disputes. Uber's recruitment practices came into question as many drivers accused the company of clever evasion of employment law.

Kalanick lurched from one PR gaffe to another. He played in celebrity circles while his drivers eked out a living. He treated them like a fungible commodity. One conflict was caught on video. He generally acted as though he were smarter and better than those around him. He once told a national magazine that because of his wealth and star status, he could find a woman on demand—"You know, like boob-er."

It all unraveled for him in 2017 when a former employee posted a 3,000-word blog describing the toxic culture at the company. Sexual harassment, it was alleged, was ignored or even encouraged. Bullying behavior tolerated if not promoted. The missive described a full-on bro culture with all the negative connotations that go with it. At the same time, the company incurred huge financial losses because of billion-dollar investments in poorly conceived business schemes, like self-driving cars. The board forced him out.

Uber has never posted a profit since its founding.

At another major tech conference in San Francisco in the fall of 2007, hotel rooms were scarce and expensive. Brian Chesky, Joe Gebbia, and Nathan Blecharczyk decided to offset some expense by renting three air mattresses in their apartment to friends. They provided breakfast, too. They built a rudimentary website a few months later and found three paying renters who signed up online for the same arrangement.

Thus, AirBed & Breakfast, Airbnb, was born.

The company exploded. In less than a decade, millions of "hosts" were renting rooms, homes, and even castles to millions of "guests." It took great care to nurture its key stakeholders, who, in addition to hosts and guests, it identified as employees, communities, and shareholders.

> I've always looked at culture as a form of intangible compensation. I've known a lot of people making very good money who told me they have Sunday-evening anxiety because they dread the coming week. When I was at ASU, I met many people who freely acknowledged they could be making 50 percent more in private industry but enjoyed the culture and being around students. This is an individual priority that shifts around at different points in your career.

In regard to its employees, Airbnb committed to a culture of diversity and belonging, to live its values each and every day, and to make the company a place where development is encouraged and commitment is rewarded. It believes a lodging company should feel like home in every aspect. The company's leaders went on record saying they consider employees family.

The company uses multiple channels to communicate with its stakeholders. Airbnb often provides free or discounted housing in local emergencies, such as when Hurricane Sandy hit New York. It is almost never in the business press, unless it's for the good it does. Its leaders don't consider themselves perfect but are known to solve sticky business problems with a dependable mix of integrity and transparency.

Airbnb is valued at more than $100 billion.

Which of these companies would you like to work for?

Which of these companies would you like to lead?

I dealt with a lot of subjectivity in my HR career, but I have found this immutable truth: the person who runs the organization sets the tone for it. They do it through the words they use and how they deliver them. They do it through what they reward or, more importantly, what they ignore. Their actions can be public and intentional or subtle and accidental. They do it by how they behave when things are going well and when things are going poorly. They do it all day, every day.

People always watch you.

We've established what effective leadership behaviors look like and the importance of being thoughtful as you assemble a team. We've seen how imperative a clear, and clearly communicated, vision is. These are all critical elements of culture. But here are a few more points you should remember as you deliberately build your workplace environment.

Talented people don't like or need a lot of rules, but the rules you do have should be consistently applied. Especially those having to do with how employees should treat one another. I can't tell you how many times I was told of a leader or employee who crossed boundaries in the workplace yet was ignored because "Well, Bob's being Bob, and Bob's pretty valuable."

Don't put up with Bob.

Talented people don't tumble off of flatbed trucks. Cultivate relationships with your team. Show interest in their physical and emotional well-being. Listen to them. Make them feel connected.

People have interests and lives outside of work. Be respectful of their time off. Quitting time is quitting time. Vacation time is vacation time. Try to rarely send anything of importance, and never anything negative, to your team on a Friday afternoon lest you impose on their weekend. This is especially true as the lines between work and home continue to blur.

Talented people can sniff out BS like a hound dog sniffs out a raccoon. Don't insult their intelligence by minimizing bad news or avoiding tough questions. Answer direct questions directly. This is the respectful thing to do.

People will claim a stake in your success if you invite them to. Show them you are helping them achieve their goals, and they will always help you reach yours.

This must be remembered: people with career options want to work in an ethical community where trust is paramount.

What will you do to build a great place to work?


## SKILL FOUR:
## MANAGING MULTIPLE PRIORITIES AND AUDIENCES

We compared individual-contributor and strategic-leader roles early in Chapter 8. The key difference was control. Leaders are less likely to be subject to an agenda because they should be *creating* the agenda. They decide where to apply their time, energy, and focus. They set speed and direction, identify desired outcomes, and develop the plan to unfold after them.

Recall that leadership roles are subject to more-intense scrutiny and have more audiences to play to and constituencies to satisfy. The demands are abundant, the problems tougher, and the pressure to deliver is greater.

This freedom is, at once, energizing and frightening. Deal with it by learning how to manage multiple priorities and adopting different communication approaches.

Google the term "Eisenhower Matrix." You'll find a simple but powerful tool often taught in project management courses that has stood up over time. Sort your demands and tasks into four broad buckets.

**Urgent and important.** These are the tasks you must perform first for obvious reasons. You may need to deal with a system failure, a supply chain disruption, a business deal coming apart, or an emergent personnel matter. These can be frustrating, unpleasant, and put you off your game. But you have to deal with them, so don't procrastinate. Like Mark Twain once said, "If it's your job to eat a frog, it's best to do it first thing in the morning."

**Urgent but less important.** Schedule when you will deal with issues in this bucket. You may want to deliver a project or program or make a hire to support the furtherance of your vision and your goals. Make a plan here. Put blocks on your calendar, and commit to following up. Persistence is required, as there will be days when you move the ball five yards and others when you move it fifty. But you must make sure the ball keeps moving.

**Less urgent but important.** Here you have the perfect chance to delegate. These items will demand less of your personal attention, so use them as developmental opportunities for your team. Refresh yourself on the evils of micromanaging. Describe the end product, set broad direction and some check-in points, and let them run.

**Less urgent and not important.** We all spend too much time on these issues for a variety of reasons. First, we often confuse activity for accomplishment so we can congratulate ourselves for being so busy. But busy doing what? Keeping the email inbox clear? Meeting for the sake of meeting? You also have personal items to attend to, like planning your next trip, checking the Twitter feed, or reading Yelp reviews for the restaurant around the corner. Not a sin to take a break from work and refresh, but too much distraction will prevent you from reaching your goals.

Managing your focus is only part of your daily challenge in senior leadership. The communication style we discussed in Part I, your verbal and nonverbal messaging, and your ability to connect become indispensable in larger roles.

You used to receive direction and information as an individual contributor. Then you turned into a conduit in your first supervisor role as these things flowed from above, through you, and to your team. An executive must be more like the hub in a wheel as communications go up, down, and across.

Master the art of brevity when dealing with the CEO or anyone who reports to her. They're busy people and like things in the form of bullet points. Preparation is key because you will only be able to maintain their attention for a short time. Give enough context to color the point you want to make or the decision you seek to obtain. Going too deep risks creating confusion or second-guessing. Scrub all data you send up the chain because mistakes will cause a loss of confidence. You're paid to master the details, after all.

Offer options whenever possible if you need a decision, and be sure to highlight the one you prefer. A short list of pros and cons is preferable if the issue is somewhat complex. Be sure to let them know you have engaged all parties on the issue. If your communication is informational only, say so. If you need a decision or any form of commitment, say this, too. List out next steps. Create the sense you are ahead of the issue because you should be.

There will be times when, despite your best efforts, an issue has gone awry. Always let the boss know because they must not hear bad news from other sources.

Be more expansive when communicating with your team. Context will be important to them because it's not likely they were involved in all discussions of the issue at hand. They may be seeing only their sliver of the pie, so explain how the decision or issue is important to the larger organizational goals. Don't move past an issue until you're satisfied all questions have been addressed. Be candid if you don't have an answer for everything.

The most critical thing to remember when communicating with your team is nature abhors a vacuum. Misinformation and rumor fill the void, so be aggressive here. Poor communication was on your list of ineffective leader behaviors for a reason.

Working on problems or programs across functions or divisions will require a new skillset. You're now dealing with peers with healthy egos like yours, and you have no formal sway over them. They have their own agendas, their own bosses to report to, and their own resource constraints and will see their department's needs as more important than yours. Their function's culture and jargon are different. Competition may be in subtle tension with collaboration.

Here we need to revisit the topics of negotiation and persuasion.

Negotiations require a counterparty and should begin with an assessment of the people involved. Time and energy invested in working relationships, even friendships, in the office pay dividends. We usually negotiate with people on one transaction, such as a car or a home purchase, and the goal is to maximize the gain. At work, you negotiate often with peer executives, so you must both press your point and preserve comity.

You share many common interests—beginning with the success of the organization—so identify those early and revisit them frequently. The challenge appears when goals and objectives aren't so common and may even conflict. These issues will require give and take. Role clarity becomes paramount. Like any negotiation process, you must decide what you can and can't live with.

Document your agreements after the horse trading concludes. Make sure you deliver on your commitments to your fellow senior leaders, and don't change them without agreement. Address any confusion and frustration directly with your negotiating partner. Transparency and trust are never more important than when you work cross-functionally.

An executive is a change agent and cannot be successful without the ability to persuade others. Go back to your strategic vision and plans. You'll find it pretty obvious you're going to have to sell some ideas, especially if you propose a distinctly different direction or you are bumping up against embedded resistance.

People aren't going to change or adopt a new way of doing business because you asked them to. You have to create a supporting story, the business case, for your important objectives. It must be easily digestible and fairly compelling. Any attempt to persuade must deal head-on with the question "What's in it for me?"

Identify critical sponsors after you have developed your talk track. These folks don't have to reside in formal leadership roles. In fact, it is best if they are seen as subject-matter experts or other informal thought leaders in the organization. Having them on your side is huge as you begin to expand the circle of those you seek to move to your point of view.

Some folks are data driven, so you have to bring the goods. Describe in quantitative terms the problem you see and the outcomes you seek. Others are more intuitive and respond to qualitative arguments, so be prepared to connect with them on an emotional level.

Refine your messages, and your base of support will grow. Share credit, and begin to sell the idea as "ours" instead of "mine." Push where you need to; pull back when you have to. Take a pause, and watch momentum build.

Of course, not every idea you have will be a winner. If your negotiation and influencing efforts are met with a profoundly underwhelming response from the good thinkers you know, it might be time to drop the idea. You can always raise it from the dead down the road.

Your world at work expands along with your responsibilities. You will quickly flail if you take on too much, misplace your focus, and can't encourage people to come along with you.

## SKILL FIVE:
## LOOKING INTO THE FUTURE

When was the last time you read a newspaper on newsprint? Worked with a travel agent to book a trip? Bought all twelve songs on the newest "album" from a favorite musician? Spent an afternoon browsing at a bookstore? Tapped out a note on a BlackBerry? When did you last smoke a Marlboro Red or drink a fully sugared Coke Classic?

Years? Never?

These and countless other industries once dominated the American economic landscape until they were reordered, or obliterated, by technology, unforeseen calamities, and changing consumer tastes.

We all know change is constant, but it's accelerating at a quickening pace. Technology has been a primary change driver since the wheel was invented, and this will never change. We are also seeing huge demographic shifts in the United States and across the globe. When you combine the effects of technology with the effects of changing demographics, you wind up with sweeping changes in politics. The old structure fragments as wealth and power distribute in new ways to new players.

A lot of this is predictable because it has happened pretty much throughout history, even though we think what we are going through is somehow unique. What actually causes change in this era is something dramatic happening every ten years or so. Look back to 9/11/2001, followed by the great recession of 2009, then by the pandemic and political upheaval of 2020. We are only beginning to realize the massive impacts of climate change.

In between these fairly predictable and cyclical shifts on the one hand and the system-shattering events on the other lie the subtle but always changing preferences of people and societies. Decisions about how to live, how many kids to have, what to eat and drink, and what to do with free time are incredibly different from twenty years ago. They will also be seen as dated twenty years from now.

I'm not here to write a treatise on the incredibly complex topic of change. I'll leave that to bigger and better minds.

I am here to say a senior leader must always anticipate what is coming over the horizon and prepare their organization for the inevitable.

Here they come again—our biases.

Leaders—people—often miss unmissable signs of pending change because they go against the grain of rigidly held beliefs. Confirmation bias. It's easier and more comforting to ignore a changing world until it's too late. New competitors are thought of as filling a boutique niche until they take over an industry. We deny tastes are changing if our tastes are not. We're stunned when our political candidate loses because everyone we know voted for him and our exclusive news channel said he had the election locked up.

We said awareness of a bias is the only way to overcome it, and this holds true here. When you are handed the steering wheel of a department, division, or company, you take the responsibility to forever scan the environment for evidence of change. You have to actively seek data refuting your perception of the current reality. Then you must look for more. At a certain point, you decide if you want to start taking it seriously.

Be thoughtful when you see change is necessary. The battled-tested SWOT analysis—strengths, weaknesses, opportunities, threats—is always useful because it gives a quick snapshot of where you are and the impediments to where you want to go. Engage more deeply in your industry groups and publications. Cultivate relationships with skeptics because their judgment is often more reliable than the defenders of the status quo. Turn the phone off, and ideate alone or with a group of creative thinkers.

Go back to your long-term plan, and rewrite it if you need to. The team you assembled? Are they up to the task? Think about what changes to your culture you need to make to prepare for a new reality. Every question should be on the table, every assumption debunked, every option explored.

We also need to revisit self-knowledge and self-awareness. Take your internal temperature frequently, and ask yourself if you are equipped to manage what's heading your way. Review your energy and interest reserves, and be sure they are sufficient for the impending task.

Here is a specific example for you. I like the softer side of HR: leadership development, organizational culture, etc. The process side, not so much. In my last role, I often joked the day I retired would be the day before we started the implementation of a new HR computer system. I was savvy enough to know up-to-date HR software was needed and would better position the organization for long-term success. But I also knew I would have been miserable overseeing such a daunting and complex project.

On the other hand, if you know you like big changes to big things, there will be no better time in your career.

You have to deal with the emotions of all involved when you commit to change. You're going to struggle against resistance even in the best of circumstances because people fear loss of control and change to routine. Books, many books, are available on the topic of change management. I'll leave it to you to go learn more. Suffice it to say any change effort you lead will require mastery of the basic leadership skills we covered earlier: decision-making, delegation, collaboration, communication, active listening, empathy, visibility, goal setting, and calmness in the storm.

Accept you may be alone in your change-management crusade, at least for a while. You're a leader now, and sometimes, it's exactly where you should be.

## SUMMARY

We've discussed the various paths to bigger jobs and what to watch for if you are promoted from within or hired from the outside. Your first senior leadership role will be packaged with a fair amount of anxiety as you say goodbye to your familiar tactical skills and evolve an executive mindset. We touched on the universally recognized effective and ineffective leader behaviors. We closed by focusing on the five core executive skills you must refine to have impact as you join the senior ranks.

Recall our goal here was not to redefine the leadership book genre. You will have the rest of your career to learn the topic, mostly through experience. You also have the whole internet at your fingertips. I only wanted to give the basics because nobody sits down with you to explain these behaviors and skills when you make a big move in your career.

As a final exercise in Part II, rate your competence and comfort level in the five skills we discussed. This will give you a quick look at where to put your future development focus.

| Critical Executive Skill | Competence/Comfort Level | | | | |
|---|---|---|---|---|---|
| | Low to High | | | | |
| Creating a Strategic Vision | 1 | 2 | 3 | 4 | 5 |
| Building a Team | 1 | 2 | 3 | 4 | 5 |
| Building a Culture | 1 | 2 | 3 | 4 | 5 |
| Managing Priorities and Audiences | 1 | 2 | 3 | 4 | 5 |
| Anticipating Change | 1 | 2 | 3 | 4 | 5 |

# PART III

# MAKE IT LAST

---------------------

"If you want to make the gods laugh, tell them your plans" is an old Yiddish proverb.

I've always liked it because it is an important reminder of how much luck—good and bad—plays a role in our lives and our careers.

You may think your career will progress up an ever-ascending and clean, linear rise: assistant director, director, assistant VP, VP, CEO. You're wrong.

Your career will zig and zag. It will go sideways at times, maybe even backwards. You will be standing on firm career ground one day only to have a massive earthquake shake it to its core the next. You will work for a new boss who likes you even less than you like him. Your industry or company, once dominant, will fade away because of new technology or changing consumer tastes. Companies sell and merge. Unforeseen personal circumstances, like a personal or family illness, will force you to abandon one path to seek another.

On the plus side, you may meet a person on an airplane who turns into an invaluable career contact. A stray phone call from an executive recruiter will drop a chance for a bigger job in your lap. Your reputation is percolating out there, and people who know people will reach out to you with opportunities you never knew existed.

Do you see any plan here?

When on your final approach in your present career, you will shake your head in wonder at how it all happened.

Let's stipulate here and now, despite everything we've talked about, you don't have total control over how things will unfold for you. This doesn't mean you should bow to the fates because there are obvious things you should avoid if you want to make it down to the runway on your own terms.

There will be times when your energy and interest will wane. You will also likely be asked to leave a role at some point. You can minimize some of this career buffeting, or at least manage how you react to it, by choosing five attitudes to reward you in work and life.

Make this career of yours last.

# CHAPTER 11

# CAREER KILLERS

——————————

want to discuss the negative stuff first. Thirty years in human resources exposed me to the lack of judgment and staggering stupidity of otherwise smart and accomplished people. I've observed endless permutations of self-destructive acts—some funny, some horrifying—all ultimately sad.

I wondered what it must be like to go home and tell your husband you lost your lucrative job for stealing or tell your wife you were fired for sexual harassment. How do you tell the kids you failed a drug test and middle-class comfort is now a shaky proposition? As life-changing as these conversations can be, they can be the easy part if a misdeed winds up in the public domain, like on the internet or even in the criminal justice system.

> I learned everyone has a public life, a private life, and a secret life. Trouble comes when your secret life is uncovered in the workplace. Keep your personal stuff miles away from your employer.

These things will kill your career every time they come to light.

## DISHONESTY

I worked at a nuclear power plant. You'll be happy to know they are the most secure places in any industry. Myriad physical security barriers exist, and highly trained, armed officers drill on various attack scenarios. Any person having access to the design or operation of the plant must undergo a background screen. These power stations share information about employees constantly through structured databases and other means.

Our plant had a half dozen or so retired FBI, Secret Service, and homicide detective types to run down rare and vague threats and conduct other minor investigations. Great guys all, though a little under-challenged.

The three-story office buildings housing support staff had kitchen galleys with little boxes near the coffeepot where we dropped our fifty cents whenever we went for a fill-up. One day, somebody noticed one of the boxes was always empty. Our plainclothes guys were fired up—finally something to do. They hung a video camera in the kitchen and taped a nuclear engineer using a pen knife to pick the lock on the box and unload the loot.

The "case" came my way as the engineer was in one of my client groups. We established he was taking five, maybe seven, dollars at a time. We had to decide what to do with him. I knew if we fired him, we would have to enter his name into one of the databases I described, and his career in the nuclear business would be over. This troubled me.

I asked my boss for his opinion. He could tell I was struggling with the decision. "Kevin," he told me, "if we can't trust him with five dollars, we can't trust him with anything worth more than five dollars."

Of course he was right, and a livelihood in nuclear power was over.

This is one of many stories I could tell about theft in the workplace. They all end the same—with the termination of an employee, the ending of a career, and destructive implications to life at home.

I've never worked for a place where theft was tolerated. It won't be tolerated where you work either.

Dishonesty takes other forms. Fraudulent requests for expense reimbursement. Saying you took a mandatory training when you didn't. Billing hours not worked on behalf of a client. Shading the truth if ever involved in a company investigation. Embellishing your accomplishments on a project, or simply not fessing up when something you were supposed to handle wasn't handled.

A less serious lie may be overlooked, and you may be able to keep your job. Still, your career where you work will be over—they just won't tell you.

## INABILITY TO CONTROL YOUR APPETITES

A director who worked down the hall from me and his wife were in the "lifestyle." This is a contemporary term for what was once called swinging, or wife-swapping. This couple had been hooking up with one of his subordinates and her husband, and the sex turned into a closer relationship than intended. I opened an email one morning from someone I did not know. It was the coworker's husband expressing concern his wife was slipping away from him and falling in love with her boss. He offered to show me pictures of the director and his wife engaged in whatever as proof, but I politely declined.

I've never been one to judge others for what they do in their private life as long as everyone is of age and consents. Except a person lower in the hierarchy can never truly provide consent in this situation. An argument can always be made the person felt they had to accede to pressure to keep the boss happy. This person had to go.

It astounds me people still don't realize the modern workplace is not forgiving of sexual escapades between leaders and employees. Despite recent social movements like #MeToo and endless rounds of training and headlines, people in power—mostly men—still think of the workplace as an appropriate place for coupling. Remember our friend from Uber? He is not the only CEO fired in recent years for fomenting a sexually charged culture. Other high-profile leaders, even iconic media types, have been let go for having a relationship with an underling.

People, I'm going to say this once: your sex life must never overlap your work life.

Drug or alcohol problems still pop up in the workplace, though not as frequently as they used to. I don't know what to attribute this to, but it's a good trend. Maybe the generations who came after the boomers drink less and are more health conscious overall.

Employers are also much more enlightened when dealing with addiction than they were in the past. If your use of drugs or alcohol has already impacted your friends, your family, and your health, it will only be a matter of time before it affects your career. Look for help. It's likely your company has resources to assist you to work through the problem.

## INABILITY TO CONTROL YOUR IMPULSES

You may be smart enough not to steal, drink, or hunt for sex during the course of your workday, but other, less-obvious behaviors can bring your career to a halt.

Doesn't it feel good sometimes to complain about the boss? Let the frustration out with whoever will listen. Maybe go for a beer with a "trusted" coworker and tag-team her demolition since misery loves company. Nice to have a release and come back to the office recharged.

It's a huge mistake to assume your feedback will not reach the boss. Your trusted coworker will tell their trusted coworkers while conveniently forgetting to mention their own participation in the pity party. Maybe this same person winds up in the boss's doghouse. There's a bus coming, and you'll soon be underneath it.

Absolutely do not say anything snarky about the boss in email or text. The message will resurface at a bad time for you.

Despite being an incompetent ogre, your boss is still human, and feelings get hurt. Feelings are also remembered. There's no reason to expect this person to continue to sponsor or support you in any way after they catch wind of your comments. Be honest; you wouldn't, either.

Keep negative opinions about the boss away from work. Share it with your significant other, if they are not tired of hearing about it yet. Mumble to your dog on the morning walk.

One option is act like an adult and share your observations with the boss herself.

Another behavior you'll see often: folks in leadership walking the halls like they are walking the plank. Remember, people are often promoted for their technical skills and not prepared to deal with the stress of a larger job. If you're not happy, it will show. Your devotion to the organization will be questioned. People will not want to work with you.

Go back to our chat about self-knowledge. Leadership is not for everyone. Be honest with yourself, and ask for a different role if you can't be a positive presence.

We spent time on bullying in the last section, so I won't hold this note too long. The top-down, up-or-out workplace culture is losing favor. What you produced was once the currency of the workplace. Equal attention is now paid to how you accomplish things. Leaders today are encouraged to serve their team, not the other way around. If you're still wagging your finger in someone's face—remember him?—start softening this edge now.

Other overt displays of emotion will be noticed, too. We said in Part I not to gloat or pout at successes or failures. Remember also your needs absolutely do not take precedence over the needs of others. Self-centered people are tagged quickly. And don't forget poorly handled stress brings negative attention.

Controversial statement alert: you may be forgiven for crying in the workplace…once.

Everything discussed here falls under the rubric of toxic behavior. It is career limiting.

## SOCIAL MEDIA PRESENCE

People always watch you.

Our elections are more contentious than ever. The United States is incredibly polarized, with half the country thinking the other half are morons. This tribalization shows no sign of abating.

Yet people on career sites like LinkedIn are still making political posts, sharing conspiracy theories, advocating for or against controversial causes, and arguing with people they don't know. Others are self-immolating on Twitter and sharing nasty memes on Facebook.

Like many, I love a good political debate, and I fall into the trap of thinking my opinion prevails because it's my opinion and no way can it be wrong.

> People believe the right to free speech extends into the workplace and they can't be discriminated against for their views. This is wrong. An employer can't make employment decisions based on race, ethnicity, age, gender, sexual identity, or disability, but the law does not speak to political orientation. Employers can take a pass on you if they disagree with your opinion or how you express it.

I also know being too public or belligerent with my thoughts on the issues of the day will only lead to alienating half of my potential employers or clients. It results in my being diminished in the eyes of others.

The negative impression you create far outlives the content of your comments, posts, and likes, which have the staying power of a wisp of candle smoke. Whose mind are you going to change anyway?

Next time you feel inspired or enraged enough to jump into the totally pointless online fray, put the phone down, and do something positive and productive instead.

# CHAPTER 12

# WHAT TO EXPECT OVER THE COURSE OF YOUR CAREER

—————————————

The average person will work in a structured setting for forty to fifty years.

I have confidence you won't sabotage yourself. You will also eventually find a career track to play to your strengths and interests. Through networking, and a little luck, you'll find a place where things feel right—more like a community than a workplace. Everything will fall into line for you, and the rhythms in your life and career will hum. This is good. This is success.

Yet a half a century is still a half a century. You're a human being and will not escape the inevitable challenges the universe tosses your way.

You will tire. You will at times be uninspired. If you push your career to the limits of what you want to achieve, ignore the signals your environment sends you, or refuse to respond to coaching, you may even be fired.

## YOU'RE FATIGUED

Physical energy gives us what we need to survive in this world. Mental energy gives us what we need to thrive. Managing energy is even more important than time because the latter becomes an endless, dull slog without the former. Granted, energy can be sapped through things like a newborn baby, stress, or illness, yet we have much more control over it than we think.

You will notice your natural energy starting to wane a bit as you go deeper into your career, no doubt because of age and the cumulative weight of increasing responsibilities.

You don't have to accept this decline. Be more astute about investing in yourself and changing your habits as the years pass.

Start by taking a look at your eating and drinking habits.

Your body's metabolism becomes less tolerant of processed foods as you age. Food manufacturers and fast-food chains spend millions finding the right mix of sugar, salt, and fat to hook you on everything packaged in a can or cellophane. Nutritionists tell us the big three are not a sustainable source of energy or satiety. Sugar, caffeine, and low-quality carbs are especially notorious for providing brief bursts of energy. The problem is the inevitable crash following their consumption.

These foods are also a source of inflammation, which is itself the source of chronic diseases like diabetes, high blood pressure, obesity, and even cancer.

Here, you are encouraged to go deep into investigation. For now, ask yourself these questions:

**Am I eating breakfast?** This most important meal of the day ignites your metabolism and jump-starts your brain—which consumes a disproportionate amount of fuel. It also prevents you from craving a Big Mac when eleven in the morning rolls around. The first meal need not be a big production. High-fiber options, like a good-quality cereal, dense fruit, or a smoothie, give your day a great start.

**Am I eating fewer, smaller meals rather than one larger meal?** This is a good strategy to keep your energy level consistent during the day. Try not to ever be too full or too hungry.

**How colorful is my plate?** We already mentioned fruit, but seek a variety of color in the form of vegetables in your daily diet, too.

**Am I a white bread person?** Transition to whole grains. In fact, you should avoid the whites—sugar, flour, and rice—altogether.

**Am I still eating a sixteen-ounce steak?** Train yourself to cut back. Doctors counsel the main animal protein in your meal should be about the size of the palm of your hand.

**How much water am I drinking?** Press down with your index finger on a meatier part of your body. You should receive some slightly doughy or spongy feedback. Up your water intake if you don't see this response.

This is how the body is fueled.

Also, take a look at how much alcohol you're drinking. Your liver will not process it as well as you turn the corner into your forties. I spent time with a work-hard, play-hard organization in my thirties, and it was not uncommon to stay out until one in the morning at a regional or national gathering, then rise for an eight-o'clock-morning-meeting start. No way would this happen now. Hangovers are more severe, the sleep more interrupted, and energy the next day nonexistent. Avoid more than two drinks a day. Drink better-quality wine, beer, and spirits when you do, but never before bedtime.

Now shoot for maximum fuel efficiency.

*Homo sapiens* have been around for about 200,000 years. Yet it has only been the last two or three generations since we've moved from the fields, farms, and factories into cubes and offices. Our bodies, built by nature for maximum movement, are horribly confused. They crave for us to provide what used to come naturally: activity.

You're a grown person and don't need reminding of the benefits of exercise. You know it will reduce your risk of the diseases I mentioned. You've been told stronger muscle and bone provide a reserve, if not a defense, against skeletal issues like back problems, joint pain, or arthritis. You are not surprised to learn your mood improves when you work out because of the physical release of endorphins and the emotional aspects of feeling better about yourself.

Every week, shoot for about 150 minutes of moderate physical activity or seventy-five minutes of high-intensity training. Strength training is good, aerobic activity is better, and a mix of the two is preferred.

The last leg of the triad for an energetic, productive body and mind is sleep.

A great sleeper most of my life, I could have medaled in it if it were an Olympic sport. I'd be asleep before my wife was done brushing her teeth. Eight and a half hours later, I'd bounce out of bed energized and enthused. Every new day brought adventure, and I would cram as much activity into it as possible.

I remember people complaining about insomnia and I thought, *Well, how bad can it be? More time to read or rewatch old favorites on TV. I wish people would stop complaining about insomnia.*

This changed in my early fifties. I had a harder time falling asleep, and when I did, I would wake up at two in the morning for no good reason. I let the problem take up full-time residence in my head, and the whole thing became a self-reinforcing problem. I started to incessantly read up on insomnia. Even took a couple of online programs. I wore a smartwatch and looked at my sleep chart the moment I woke up. I started to fear going to bed because I knew torture awaited.

Weeks of this turned into months. My energy evaporated. I was living life looking through a Vaseline-smeared glass pane, only vaguely in tune with what was happening around me. Things I used to love and look forward to, like a public speaking gig at work, flying a glider on a weekend, or a dinner date with friends, became subjects of much dread, even anxiety. Depression set in—insomnia and depression are almost always linked, but you can never tease out which is the chicken and which is the egg. I almost stopped functioning.

To make a very long story short, I eventually discovered I had an age-related hormonal problem. I began to take a supplement, under a doctor's supervision, and things came back to balance. With balance came a return to normal life. I was soon blasting blues music on the way to work while drinking in the beauty of the mountains surrounding Phoenix. The nightmare ended.

Please know insomnia and other severe sleep problems are not natural and are usually treatable. You may have to make adjustments, like less wine and screen time and more exercise. You may need to see a doctor for a sleep apnea test. Don't accept poor sleep; keep trying until you find a workable solution. Then guard your sleep as if it were a treasure, because it is.

Master this mix of diet, exercise, and sleep as you age. You'll feel better about the world and your place in it.


## YOU'RE UNINSPIRED

*Ennui* is a French term defined as a feeling of being bored and mentally tired, usually caused by having nothing interesting or exciting to do.

I assume you have an above-average drive at work and home. You are an intellectually curious type who finds inspiration and motivation in taking on new challenges. You thrive on solving problems. Pleasure comes to you when you take a step back and look at what's been accomplished. Even though you don't like to gloat, you do like to win.

There will come a time when some or all of this psychic reward goes missing. Maybe you have been in the role too long, all the low-hanging fruit has been picked, and working on the big issues feels like climbing a sand dune. You find yourself feigning interest in project meetings, or you have to scrape around to find a new idea. Something is off. You're flat. People ask if everything is okay. The mojo stopped working.

What to do?

First, review your general physical and mental health. Check in on your progress on the lifestyle changes we discussed. Assure yourself a mild depression has not set in. If you're satisfied the body and mind are solid, and things outside work are good, start a game plan with a mix of the following strategies.

Reevaluate your goals. You won't make meaningful progress against any of them if you have too many. No satisfaction can be found while surrounded by half-finished projects. Their presence can actually scream failure. No wonder you don't feel like going to work.

If your goals are too large, you won't start on them. They will emerge to the top of your inbox and hover there until something less intimidating floats by to take their place. Months or maybe years will pass, and you will quietly accept the unrealistic, and unrealized, goal will never be completed. Dispiriting for sure, yet oddly empowering, as you've now released energy to apply elsewhere.

Though it sounds counterintuitive, pare back and clarify what you are committed to so you can recover a sense of accomplishment. Shoot for a rolling average of three to five objectives to support your final desired outcome, the charter you created. Make them SMART: specific, measurable, actionable, relevant, and time-bound. This way you can put some points in the win column and recapture momentum.

Your boss is not going to like me for saying this, but work fewer hours. High-drive types like you take misplaced pride in working fifty, sixty, or even seventy hours a week. Except the additive hours don't equate to additive productivity. Going past fifty hours in a work week is impacting your ability to manage your emotions and pick up cues your environment, and the people in it, may be sending your way.

Judgment suffers as a result of this routine, so you're also making mistakes you'll have to fix during tomorrow's twelve-hour day. It's creating a vicious cycle because you now have stress at home to go along with your stress at work and no safe harbor in which to relax. No pleasurable activity remains after such an investment of time. Boredom can be the only result.

Reignite relationships when ennui takes hold. Reconnect with your power mentors to check in on what they are up to or ask for their advice. Develop new relationships with people you find motivating or interesting. Every work week presents ten chances to connect socially with people: five mornings for breakfast/coffee and five for lunch. Shoot for a couple of outings every week so you can have something to look forward to. It has been validated many times that having friendships at work promotes your overall engagement.

Become more active in your professional associations. Opportunities abound to contribute outside your normal work-day on boards or committees. You can also appropriate—the HR word for "steal"—ideas you hear from peers in other companies. Conferences out of town can be animating. A nice trip to a place you've never been. A full agenda of interesting speakers. New contacts from different regions of the country. You almost always return from these trips with renewed purpose and vigor.

Boredom in this big, wonderful, interesting world is not natural. Nature is trying to signal your need for balance. We're going to discuss this more later.

## YOU'RE FIRED

Most energetic, visionary, creative, and opinionated professionals have one thing in common. They've likely been fired.

Motivational speakers and the internet are full of inspirational stories of the career setbacks of people like Abe Lincoln, Oprah

Winfrey, or Steve Jobs. My favorite is Walt Disney being told by a newspaper publisher he had no talent for drawing cartoons. These oft-told tales have, at their core, a clueless person or organization failing to see the brilliance of the folks to whom they are giving the boot. The protagonist finds vindication by earning billions of dollars or having a monument built in their name.

This is almost never the case, though, and reasons for being let go vary in real life. Most HR people will tell you skills get you hired, but personality gets you fired. The person failed to respond to coaching, misread the moment in the organization, or simply exhausted everyone around them.

But really good people can be fired, too. Politics can play a role, as sometimes people land on the right side of the right issue but the wrong side of the wrong person. There may have occurred an appalling level of ineptitude, and a head has to roll to appease an external audience—even if the person fired worked on the periphery. A senior person can cause a mess, then push blame onto a more-junior leader. The term CYA stays in the lexicon for a reason.

A talented person can simply be in a wrong role. The organization puts them in center field when they should play catcher and wants to bench them when they can't run down fly balls in the gap.

I once heard a consultant say, "Unless you are prepared to leave an organization, you can never lead an organization." I took this to mean if you don't stand behind some kind of conviction, you'll never have the courage to fully realize your ambitions, vision, and plans. An executive can be hired to make change in an organization, then the organization decides it likes the status quo after all. The change agent is pushed out. A lot of good people lose jobs this way.

The most common reason of all for losing a job is quite pedestrian. You are caught up in some kind of a downsizing, reorganization, or merger.

Here is what to do when asked to leave, told your upward career has no more up, cut for financial reasons, or assigned the dreaded "special projects" role.

Stay calm. You're standing in a hole, and you must not dig. Resist making a bad situation worse by tossing out empty threats of litigation. The firing manager already spoke to the corporate counsel, and she signed off. Plus, litigation is only successful in extreme cases and typically a waste of money and energy. Your court case can come up on a Google search, too.

Don't create an emotional scene because it is undignified, will be the last thing you are remembered for, and will be regretted down the road. It may be hard to find the restraint, but these behaviors take you nowhere. If you had any self-awareness at all, you secretly knew this moment was coming anyway.

Think this through, as another obvious reason exists to keep your cool. You may need at least a neutral reference from these folks soon.

People always watch you.

Take this shot to your chin, then shake your head to clear your mind a bit.

You must keep your wits because now it's time to negotiate. If you're being offered three months' severance pay, try to negotiate your way to six. Make sure you ask for the pro-rated bonus. Ask for accommodation if your stock options or retirement are close to vesting. Healthcare is critical, so you must nail down as much coverage as you can for as long as you can.

You may not think you have leverage here, but you do. The person firing you is not at all comfortable and wants to salve their own guilt by "seeing what they can do." Use their shame to your advantage. You may not seal the deal in this initial conversation, but you have at least opened a path.

Here, you must also ask for feedback on why things went wrong. Not in an argumentative or defensive way. The decision is not going to change. Nobody has ever unfired someone in the moments after they fired them. Again, you're trying to maintain a dialogue and show a little professionalism.

This is important because soon you must reflect on what happened and what you may have done to cause this predicament. Think of being fired as breaking up with a spouse or significant other. As much as we like to tell ourselves it was entirely the other person's fault, the reality is we shared some of the blame. When your powers of reason return, you're going to have to take a critical look in the mirror so you don't wind up here again. More on this soon.

You will go through the steps of the grieving process when you lose your job unexpectedly. Anger is the one to watch out for, as it is the most corrosive emotion of all and will prevent you from moving on to other opportunities—and there *will* be countless other opportunities. Again, more soon.

Though you won't see it in the days or weeks following, your firing will not be the worst thing to ever happen to you. Go back to our heartwarming anecdotes; it may actually be a good thing. You may have been waiting for somebody to make up your mind for you, and you can now do a long-planned career reinvention. At most, it will be a footnote in the story of your career.

# CHAPTER 13

# FIVE IMPORTANT ATTITUDES

———————————

We've talked about tactics, strategies, behaviors, and skills. We shift now to a discussion of attitudes—the state of mind you bring to work and to life.

Attitudes can be ephemeral: short-lived, emotional responses to specific environments, obligations, situations, things, or people. My attitude goes negative when presented with a staggering bill for wee portions of sushi at a Japanese restaurant. People who keep me waiting give me an attitude. The Dallas Cowboys…fuhgeddaboudit. Thankfully, these annoyances pass quickly.

Sustained attitudes have a more lasting impact on how we interact with the world. These belief systems often precondition us, indeed lead us, to both positive and negative outcomes. We have more choice over how we cultivate them since they're constant and less fleeting. You can intentionally commit to an attitude by deciding you want to approach life a certain way.

The successful people I've met made the conscious choice to be entrepreneurial and accountable in the way they manage their careers. They treat their vocations and lives as exciting journeys full of new experiences. They know not everyone obtains everything they want in life, and they're cool with it. People who tread lightly upon this Earth are grateful for where they are in life and believe nothing good, or bad, lasts forever. They see money as an avenue to comfort and status but stay more interested in the independence it brings. Being known as a good person is their most-sought reward.

Behaviors can change. Skills can improve. Attitudes can be chosen.

Consider the following, and decide the state of mind you'll bring to every new morning.


## ACTIVELY MANAGE YOUR CAREER

Sailboats have always interested me. They're so effortless as they glide across the water. Few impediments exist to how far they can go, as they have no gas tank to refill and few mechanical parts to fail. A good sailor easily goes from point to point under all but the most extreme conditions, even against a strong headwind. They do this by keeping their sails trimmed correctly. They make periodic tweaks—letting line out here, cranking line in there—as they respond to changing wind velocities and direction. Making no adjustments would lead to aimless drift—the doldrums.

Like sailing, you must do basic things to keep on the right track so you realize your potential. You'll need to accept tweaks to your career—like adjusting a sail to keep it full of wind—are demanded up to the day you pull into port.

Check your direction periodically. The calendar moves by fast, and family or financial obligations remain always at the fore. You'll begin to wander from your destination. But you must remember you follow the chart you create for yourself, and nobody is going to come along and tap you on the shoulder when you go off course.

Think in terms of waypoints and time. You should look three to five years into the future at every stage of your career.

Say you are a director and want a VP role. You may be able to see the path clearly from where you are. But what if you can't? The person whose job you aspire to may not be going anywhere soon. Maybe you are less tenured than her other, most-likely successor anyway. All the dominoes would have to fall the right way for you to be promoted. You may have to seriously consider leaving a perfectly good situation to advance. Start planning a strategic career move now. Go back to the basics of presence, reputation management, profile building, and, of course, networking.

Check your gut periodically. Different things will be important to you at different times in your life. Generally, you'll be experimenting and seeking in your thirties, settling and earning in your forties, and trying to remove as much work BS from your work life as you can in your fifties.

It follows, then, if you are in early career and experience extended ennui or you can't commit to your current career choice, it might be time for a tweak. It is more difficult to make significant change as you age.

Your financial obligations typically peak in your forties as the new, large house needs furnishing and the kids need educating. It's pretty easy to do an internet search of what your job is worth in the labor market. If you think you're undercompensated and should be doing better, it might be time for a tweak, as big pay leaps in the same position at the same company are not common. Again, think "waypoints" because significant new opportunities become scarcer after you turn fifty.

As far as your fifties go, they are a topic for another book. Suffice it to say, after years of striving and politics and competition and starting anew, finding a place where you enjoy the day-to-day and like and trust your colleagues is reward enough.

Check your values periodically to see if they are still aligned with your employer's. You should be proud of their products, proud of the way they participate in the community, proud of the way they treat the planet, and proud of the way they treat their employees. Do you still trust the CEO and her team? Do you see diversity in the senior ranks or on the board? If any of these things concern you, it might be time for a tweak.

Check your brain periodically. Make sure you are being stretched at work and at home. Press hard, and always be a learner. Take advantage of every formal and informal learning opportunity your current employer offers. Pay attention to the good leaders in the organization to adopt their effective habits. Pay attention to the crappy leaders in the organization so you can consciously avoid bad habits. If you aspire to a larger job in your organization or industry and you know intuitively you've learned all you can in your current gig, time for a tweak.

Lifestyle issues outside of work play a big role, too. I know I've taken a pass at several intriguing opportunities because they were in places I would not want to live. But another phone call always seemed to come. They will for you, too.

Of course, you are not making these assessments in a vacuum. If you have a family, they may appreciate being involved in a career decision. And they deserve to be involved.

So many factors deserve consideration when you reach a career crossroads. Here are a few more.

Blue-chip companies are great to have on your résumé early in your career. A level of panache—implicit bias?—is attached to having experience at companies like Google, Amazon, GE, Procter & Gamble, PepsiCo, and others. Executive recruiters keep databases, and you will come up in a lot more searches as they source candidates if you've worked at one of these well-known companies. So even if you're not ready to make a lifelong commitment to them, and even if you can make more at generic brand X, I always recommend doing a three-to-five-year stint at high-profile places if you have the opportunity. It will slingshot your career.

> Like cottage cheese, your tenure in a senior job has a shelf life. The game and the players change over time. Even coaches who win championships are often gone within a few years. Better to leave a job with a nice send-off than to have to clear your office in thirty minutes. Know when to stay and when to leave.

It's tempting to stay at a place that meets 80 percent of your emotional, intellectual, and financial needs. Nobody will think less of you if you decide it's good enough. If the destination on your chart is not closer after a bit of time, or is even receding from view, the reality is you're going to have to make a decision to unfurl the mainsail and go. You may fail. Big deal. Other opportunities will pop up. My experience dealing with senior leaders is they all went all-in at one point in their career.

You, only you, are accountable for how the boat is steered.


## BE RESILIENT

I opened this section of the book by pointing out your career will be long and filled with ups and downs. Even if you avoid professional suicide, which we now know you will, the universe is still going to send a nasty fastball across your chin every now and then to keep you humble.

Surviving and learning from missteps or misfortunes is known as resilience. You're going to need to dip into a well of mental toughness several times, probably multiple times, in your life and career. Here are a few ways to keep it replenished.

I see two elements of resilience: the emotional and the analytical.

Perspective is key. Think back to our conversation about calmness in the storm when we said what keeps you up all night today will be forgotten in a month. Resilient people take setbacks in stride because they see them for what they are: temporary. They also frame them against the worst-case scenario and realize, absent loss of life or limb, most everything can be fixed. They may take a deep gulp after something unpleasant happens and sardonically say to themselves, "Well, that was fun," but then they look for what's next. Smart thing to do.

What's not smart is holding on to things you cannot change. The worst thing to do when you are treated unfairly, passed over for hire or promotion, or make a preventable, costly mistake in the workplace or in life is to continue to relive the incident. This is like replaying an endless video loop in your head, except there will be no new happy ending after the upsetting scenes, only more of the same upsetting scenes. It's called rumination, and it is not healthy. It saps your energy, takes you out of the present, and can prevent you from moving on.

Do you create secret revenge fantasies for those who have done you wrong? Has it occurred to you while thinking about that person in the moments before you are not falling asleep, they are happily snoozing away?

Resentment is like taking poison and waiting for the other person to die.

Similarly, don't take out your anger at any given situation on anyone not related to the situation. Your significant other, kids, dog, and friends did not cause a work or career problem, so they should not be paying the price for it. Don't bleed on people who did not cut you.

I am not saying to forgive people who worked you over. Forget them.

After you learn to accept, analyze.

I was waiting for a flight, and a rambunctious boy of about five was jumping from chair to chair, running in front of people, and otherwise creating havoc in the gate area. He ultimately wound up splayed on the floor crying with a slightly cut lip.

"Billy," an elderly woman I assumed was his grandmother said with a pleasant drawl, "everything happens for a reason, and mostly the reason is you're not too smart."

The woman had a PhD in wisdom.

Overcome confirmation bias, and evaluate evidence you over-looked on the way to your recent setback. Think back to some of the biggest mistakes you ever made. It's likely others were trying to warn you about being on the wrong path. Maybe you knew your behavior was risky, like seeking sex at work, but thought you were immune from consequences. You may have failed to hold a tricky decision to your nose to see if it smelled and went against your intuition.

I've said this several times now. The reason you must analyze your failures is so you do not repeat them. It's a short haul from victim of circumstances to volunteer.

One more point on resilience: mental calmness. Have you ever watched a dog on a leash yanking its owner all over the place only to see another person walk by with a pooch happily padding at her heel? Think of your mind as the dogs. What kind of mind do you want? One fighting and pulling you? Or one in harmony with you? All of us can benefit greatly by learning to calm our minds through breathing, yoga, or meditation. Pursue these if an unquiet mind is impacting your quality of life.

Keeping things in perspective, letting things go, and objectively learning from negative situations keep you more balanced—and happy. Other elements of resilience have already been discussed. Having goals helps fuel motivation when times are tough. Great friends and mentors will pull you through and help you rebound from even the greatest setbacks. A strong and well-rested body makes life better when things are good and at least tolerable when you hit a speed bump.

Keep moving forward. Life is in your windshield, not the rearview mirror.


## KEEP YOUR IDENTITY

I am not going to lie; having influence and standing at work is pretty cool. Your emails and phone messages are answered more quickly. You notice people becoming deferential to you. You receive compliments on your outfit of the day. Jokes met by eye rolls from your kids evoke robust laughter in the staff meeting because people like seeing the boss happy. You puff your chest out a little more when you answer the inevitable "What do you do for work?"

Little perks give way to semi-extravagances if you are in a position to spend company money or sign contracts with vendors. Now, you have access to expensive gift baskets at holiday time, dinners at Morton's The Steakhouse, concert tickets, and invitations to suites at athletic events. Pretty heady stuff.

It's illusory and temporary.

I was once in a position to recommend approval for our contracts with health insurance companies and investment options for our 401(k) plan. I received much largesse when it was time to renew. In fact, my one time in a private jet was when a health-plan company flew me back to Connecticut for a sales pitch. Money managers from back east came to Phoenix, almost always in February and never in July, for short portfolio reviews and long golf afternoons.

When the company I worked for sold, I took a severance package and spent a few months knocking around. I called some of these folks who loaded me down with goodies when I decided to reenter the job market to ask them to be on the lookout for me. To network.

In some cases, I answered warm return phone calls.

With others, I heard only crickets. As I was no longer in a position to help them, they had no reason to help me. I was not surprised, as by this time, I had become a pretty astute observer of human nature and a little bit cynical. But it can be jarring if you're not ready for it.

Nobody stays in a job forever, and you won't either. Best to prepare yourself for the day when your business card has a little less weight.

Understand and accept this concept of borrowed equity. The attention you receive, at least in some measure, is coming from people who want something from you. Be hyper-alert to this; don't take it for granted or think it will never go away. A corollary here is to never be abusive with it.

It might be a good idea to find other sources of fulfillment if your whole identity is wrapped up in your job title.

This can include spreading some of the power and experience around to benefit people outside your company. Look for ways to make use of your access to resources and influence to help your community and those less fortunate. Think about the conversation we had about participating on nonprofit boards. Consider other ways to contribute in less-structured ways. Volunteer at a local school from time to time. Take on a mentee.

Build relationships with people outside of work, and look for ways to trade favors and connect folks—not in a mercenary or selfish way, but to plant positive karma out in the ether. Serving others is never a bad investment.

If you don't have hobbies or interests outside of work, find some now. I've mentioned being a pilot. Pilots always mention being a pilot. This was a long-standing goal I had for years, and when I turned forty, I decided to go for it. Find an interest where you can lose yourself. Blow it out. Then look for another one.

This sounds ghoulish, but scan obituaries every now and then. Usually, the reference to what the deceased did for work is pretty short. The balance of the obit is focused on the person's interesting activities and travels. Many describe deep and lasting relationships built over years. Those people who served in the military, participated in civic organizations, organized car clubs, started salsa dancing groups, or coached Little League draw my eyeballs. So do those people with radically disparate careers. This is where the richness of life resides.

Don't wait for the day when your work identity is surrendered or, worse, taken from you before you're ready. You can go from *Who's Who* to "Who's he?" in the time it takes to read this chapter. Think of ways now to live a balanced and rich life. Decide now how you want to be defined outside of your work role.


## DEVELOP FINANCIAL LITERACY

A group of us, including the CEO, were walking to lunch one day when one of my colleagues excitedly asked us to come look at his new car. "I cashed in some stock options," he said, "and I worked the dealer down to $30,000."

"Nope," the boss said, "you spent 100,000 on it because that's the value the options will have when we're done with the stock price."

The company sold a few years later at a premium price, and the boss turned out to be right. The car is in a junkyard now, and the 100,000 invested in Apple or Amazon two decades ago…the mind boggles.

I've come across well-compensated people who could not tell you the difference between a stock and a bond, who set up their 401(k) allocations at hire and never went back to adjust them, who outspent their $300,000 annual salary, and who looked totally befuddled when I explained the nuances of a nonqualified deferred compensation arrangement.

Our society generally does a poor job of preparing us to be money managers. Basic financial concepts are rarely taught in high school or college, and most of us are left to learn as we go. Many smart people actively avoid the subject of personal finance because they find it boring or intimidating, or they don't want to admit to themselves they don't understand it.

This is one of life's unsolvable mysteries.

The purpose of work for 99.99 percent of us is to make enough money to pay our bills and save enough money so we don't have to work anymore or have the option to do what we truly want to do. We should all excel at this basic life skill.

Becoming proficient in personal finance reduces financial worries at any income level. This makes life better. More importantly, having a financial cushion means you'll never have to make a career decision later in life based solely on dollars. You want to avoid having to stay in a job because you can't afford to leave.

You should be forever building toward independence through the course of your working years.

Our time is winding down, and there still exists much to learn on this topic that we can't explore now. Here are the most important things to consider early in your career.

Understand the difference between an investment and an expense.

Anything gaining value after you buy it is an investment and should be folded into your overall wealth picture as early as you can. Real estate of all kinds generally appreciates in value over time, especially in areas of above-average economic activity. These gains can be magnified if you use leverage wisely. Well-selected stocks, bonds, or mutual funds historically increase, too.

Moving vehicles, like cars, boats, RVs, and airplanes, invariably decrease in value the longer you hold them. They also need maintenance and insurance. Jewelry, most art and collectibles, and expensive electronics almost always lose value, despite what the salesperson tells you. Excepting cars, these items also have marginal or sporadic utility. They are expenses, the opposite of investments.

Of course, you work hard and should be able to enjoy the finer things in life, the luxuries bringing pleasure and signaling status, if that's important to you. I enjoy a great car with power. And you don't need my approval to buy the newest iPhone the same day it's released.

Except, if too much of your money is going to things losing value—expenses—and not enough is going to assets increasing in value—investments—you're going to put yourself, and maybe your relationships, under stress regardless of how much you make. Especially if you're borrowing or cashing in stock options to buy the shiny toys. Most people don't realize this until it's too late.

Too late because of another poorly understood concept: using the power of time to help you build wealth. The internet is full of charts and calculators on this topic. But here is an easy example.

Jane is thirty and saves $2,000 a year in a basic stock index fund for thirty-five years. Assuming an historical 8 percent annual rate of return, her nest egg at age sixty-five will be close to $400,000.

John waits until he's forty to start saving his $2,000. At the same rate of return, he will have about $200,000 at the same age.

Jane saved an extra $20,000 between age thirty and forty but wound up with $180,000 more at sixty-five.

This is the power of using compounding returns over time. Time is your best friend in wealth creation. But how many people do you know who understand this?

Financial advisers stress you should participate fully in your retirement account as soon as you start working and leave it alone until you retire. The only exception to this rule is if you need a down payment on a house because you are trading one appreciating asset for another. You still may have to pay a penalty depending on the tax laws in place when you make a withdrawal.

Back to this concept of ownership as a wealth-building strategy. Strive to own at least a piece of the organization paying you.

This may take the form of sole ownership of your own company. If owning your own firm isn't your thing, you can still obtain a bite of the action through instruments such as the aforementioned stock option. It's also common for professionals in law, medicine, engineering, or consulting to form partnerships or similar joint-ownership arrangements to share profits annually.

If you work for a smaller company that is neither a corporation nor a partnership, you still may be able to negotiate a fraction of the enterprise if you ask the owners. This is especially true if you are a key employee they don't want to lose.

The takeaway in all this is participation in ownership will move you more quickly toward your wealth goals because we all have a tendency to spend what shows up in the paycheck every two weeks—after your 401(k) deduction, right? Annual profit participation or sharing the proceeds of a sale of a company creates the cushion. Remember this when you are evaluating job offers or negotiating the terms of your promotion.

Understanding the difference between investments and expenses, using time to create wealth, and seeking ownership shares are only a few of the basics of what you should know about personal finance. We can't capture it all in a short section of a short book.

This must be emphasized: develop a positive attitude toward money management. Embrace the topic; don't hide from it. Learn early and often. Your goal should be independence from, not subservience to, your possessions or your employers.

You'll be the caretaker of your money until the day you die, so decide now you want to become good at it.


## CREATE YOUR LEGACY

You're known for what is said about you between the commas.

Jackie Robinson, who broke Major League Baseball's color barrier, was born in rural Georgia.

Bette Davis, an unconventional-looking leading lady known for stubborn perfectionism, received ten Oscar nominations for Best Actress.

Frida Kahlo, a brilliant Mexican artist who created haunting self-portraits, did not live to see her forty-eighth birthday.

These three historical figures led interesting lives in and outside their chosen professions. They changed the status quo every time they encountered it, redefining how second base was played, how genuine emotion was brought to a role, and how to convey internal pain through color on canvas. They also reordered the politics in their respective eras and opened paths for others. Multiple biographies have been written about all three.

Yet they are still primarily known for how I briefly described them.

You will be known by how others briefly describe you after you've passed through their workplaces or their lives. What do you want them to say in the half second when the sentence pauses?

Give serious consideration to this question of your legacy. Here are a few suggestions to provoke your thinking:

**A person who improved things.** There's something impressive about those who are adept at making things better. Turning a poor-performing department or company around is inherently satisfying and brings incredible value to your employer. Mentoring long-ignored talent can change the career trajectory of the people you lead.

I've noticed people with this attitude carry this drive outside of work, too. They're active within the community and generous with time and money for causes they find important. They don't just rail against what they see on the news and wait for somebody to fix things. They find meaningful ways to engage.

So many opportunities to take on; so many people to touch. Revel in this challenge to leave things better than you found them wherever you go. People will notice the difference when you move on.

**A fair and ethical competitor.** Our capitalist society is built on competition. Companies compete to take more market share or create new technologies or products. People compete with each other for promotion opportunities and the wealth that comes with them. This is good; it drives innovation on a societal scale and evokes our drive for self-actualization on an individual level.

We all must adhere to a contract for our system to work. If we believe we live in a meritocracy, we should also agree everyone should play by the same rules.

Nobody begrudges a winner if the company or person simply outhustled everyone else. Those people are often venerated. Yet everyone has a negative reaction to those who cut corners to win. Those people are often reviled. It's one reason Willie Mays was a national sports hero and Barry Bonds, with his *alleged* use of performance-enhancing drugs, will not be in the Hall of Fame anytime soon.

Strive to use your talents and skills to win within the bounds of agreed-to norms, and you'll be remembered with respect tinged with a measure of awe.

**A person who was kind.** The best legacy of all. You've been blessed with intelligence, education, good judgment, ambition, and opportunity. These attributes will combine to propel your career and life to places you can't imagine. You're going to realize your goal of being a leader or an executive. The path may be circuitous, but that's half the fun.

You'll also be empathetic toward people you encounter along the way who may not have your gifts. This will make you tolerant with those who differ from you, patient with those less talented, and humane and helpful with those going through trials.

You'll smile at a baby you see at the grocery store, tell the parents how cute she is, and watch them beam. You'll be the person who leaves the last cookie in the breakroom for someone else. You'll be kind to the planet by picking up your messes and grabbing an extra handful of litter someone else may have left behind. You'll be gentle and forgiving to yourself because you're trying your best, and you're doing a heck of a job at it.

Of all the things, both good and bad, people can say about you, why not have them say you're a nice person?

These are my ideas for being remembered. What are yours?

You've been prepared now for what to expect over the long haul. Influence your future as much as you can through preparation, perseverance, and good judgment. Spend the majority of your career and life in the moment while keeping an optimistic eye on the future. The past is there for good memories and good experiences, not to rehash what cannot be changed.

Thank the fates when they shine on you. Thank them when they don't. Renew and refresh when your body and mind are poking at you for attention. Reinvent yourself when you have to and when you don't have to.

Choose to embrace the leadership life you want for yourself.

# SUMMARY

—————————

Our afternoon together has come to an end.

My goal was to give real, clear advice on landing and leading a life in leadership.

I didn't want to confuse you with deep, esoteric, and marginally useful insights or diagrams. You wouldn't have made it this far into the book. I didn't want to pump you full of inspirational bromides found in motivational memes from Facebook and LinkedIn. They may be thought-provoking but have no staying power.

I don't think I ever claimed the tactics and strategies discussed were the only trail to your professional summit. But I have seen consistent elements in successful people in my forty years in management, observations I hope you thought worth sharing.

First, I took away some of the mystique around receiving the invitation to play at the next level in your organization or industry.

You already knew about the power of the first impression, reframed here as confirmation bias. You received a heads-up on the effects of similarity bias, and I put you on notice you will have to work a little harder for acceptance if you don't quite fit the mold of those around you. I reminded you the content of your character can be obscured, at least initially, by people looking at you through their own tainted lenses.

Happily, you now know it's not difficult to overcome these biases in the people who make the decisions over the direction of your career if you stick to the basics. Make it your goal to present yourself a bit more professionally than your current role demands. Remind yourself good health begets good energy, which begets positive attention. Take your eyes off the phone and stay in the moment with people you interact with—the young man behind the counter in the lobby coffee shop, the CEO at the next all-hands meeting—because you will be remembered.

Don't be shy about telling key people you want to advance. Seek opportunities to shine by exuding a little more confidence than people may expect. If you have an opinion on a critical topic at work, put it out there with a little oomph. It's one reason you're paid and one way to stand out. Become known as a player. Sign up for the hard task, then keep cool and make good decisions as you work through the challenge. Master the art of holding an audience. You got this; I know you do.

Be cognizant always, be intentional daily, and never lose focus on relationships. The big job will come.

When it does, step into the responsibility that comes with it. You're going to have self-doubt because we all do. There will be fewer people around to tell you what to do or how to do it, which, for me, was always the point. Quickly transition to the executive mindset.

Let go of the tactical because the team you painstakingly

assembled has it covered. They aren't looking to you to browbeat them into doing their job your way. They're hoping you give meaty work, quality feedback, clear communication, and attainable goals. They want to win. Everybody wants to win. After the win, a pat on the back will always be remembered.

While you start their hands humming, enroll their minds and guts in your vision, your charter. Communicate the plan, communicate it again, and then…communicate it one more time.

You have a near-sacred responsibility to create a positive culture. People are going to give you forty to fifty hours of their time every week, so make it enjoyable, at least as enjoyable as work can be. They want equitable treatment. Though they might not tell you, they are also looking to you to cull the toxic from the herd.

You sit in the cockpit, and their expectation is you're looking over the horizon for obstacles and opportunities.

They want to be proud of working for the company and for you. They never want to see the organization in the news, unless it's something positive. They don't want to see you bend rules. You're an ethical person; I know you are.

This leadership thing can be pretty consuming and can take your focus away from who you are at your core. Avoid mixing your personal and professional lives because you know how destructive it is for you and your loved ones if you have a lapse in judgment.

The more likely challenges for you over the long haul will be to keep your interest level high and your body and mind steeled. Remember to adapt your habits as you age and take on more responsibility at work and at home. When something goes awry, take your lumps, take your learnings, pick yourself up, and move on.

Accept you are the person most responsible for your career until you decide to end it. As you pile up the successes, don't forget being an executive is only a portion of your life; it is not who you are. Share the psychic and material wealth and experience that come with power and influence with your community.

Your work and home lives will be good for you if you expect them to be. Having a financial cushion will take away one of life's biggest stressors and open options for you. The kindness you throw out always loops back to you.

One last exercise for the future.

You will evolve from the young up-and-comer with potential to the successful, sage mentor. This will take a couple of decades and the blink of an eye. You will be admired by others for what you accomplished and how you handled yourself because people always watch you. You'll be approached by a younger person one day, and they will ask you, tentatively, how you did it.

Spend part of an afternoon and tell them.

# ACKNOWLEDGMENTS

---

I've been blessed with a varied and interesting career. A scrawny boy from the desert with a full head of hair and a new family went looking for his place in life decades ago and found it. Some hard work, preparation, networking, resilience, and luck all played a role. So did a few key people along the way.

Mike Gantt interviewed a clueless young man who knew nothing about what was then called "personnel" and saw something. He gave me a chance and gave me a career. I always look forward to seeing you, Mike, because you are generous with your wisdom.

Armando Flores was there several times with a phone call pointing me in an intriguing direction. I like to emulate his light touch with people, his enthusiasm for life, and his dedication to his community. Oh, he gives great wardrobe advice, too.

Chip Weil at Central Newspapers was a whip-smart and good-humored man with a deep understanding of his industry. I have no idea why he thought I could be a VP in newspapers, since my only industry experience was my first job delivering them, but he did, and my family and I benefitted immensely.

Morgan Olsen at ASU was always a consummate professional and a great partner on a lot of solid work.

I give gratitude to every person I had the privilege of leading over the years. I learned so much more from you than you did from me.

Toni, you have been a solid partner through it all. You and Adriana and Alana were my motivation to be my best.